Praise for 95 Power Principles

"Nelson Wolff started his long career in public service at the capitol in Austin. Fortunately for the citizens of San antonio and Bexar County, he later focused on municipal government. His *95 Power Principles* should be on the reading list of every aspiring local politician who wants to avoid learning the hard way."
—*Joe Straus, former Speaker of the Texas House of Representatives.*

"In *95 Power Principles*, Judge Wolff showcases such proactive and incisive servant leadership with his characteristic wit and honesty. This is a book and these are the principles with which I will teach future leaders."
—*Jill Fleuriet, Professor of Anthropology, University of Texas at San Antonio.*

"Those following in his footsteps have a new gift with this book. It is a well-written guide to success and failure and the appropiate use of power based on his many years of experience, his wins and losses, and that great instinct he has for service. It is just like Judge Wolff to keep giving back to us, even after he's left office."
—*Kirk Watson, Mayor of Austin and former Texas State Senator*

"An essential read for anyone interested in the governance of cities and counties. A great 'good governance' handbook for any serious leader."
—*John Montford, former State Senator and Chancellor of Texas Tech University System*

"An entertaining and insightful book on how political leadership works at the local level – and all levels, for that matter. Many of the principles also apply to running a major corporation."
—*Edward Whitacre, former CEO of AT&T and General Motors*

"During the COVID pandemic, Judge Wolff's leadership style, smarts, and work ethic were an inspiration to me and helped save countless lives across Texas. This entertaining and informative book lays out the blueprint to become, and excel as, an elected public servant in local government."
—*Travis County Judge Andy Brown*

"Nelson Wolff is a legend in local government. His advice is highly valuable and forged from a lifetime of servant leadership."
—*Dallas County Judge Clay Lewis Jenkins*

"I admire Nelson Wolff as the gold standard for public servants. His focus, throughout his career, doing the right thing for the right reasons, all the time. This book reveals how leadership should be exercised."
—*Eric Johnson, Mayor of Dallas*

"*95 Power Principles* offers a roadmap to effective leadership in the public sector, and serves as inspiration. Judge Wolff infuses the book with genuine passion in public service and reminds us of the profound impact that dedicated leaders can have in our society."
—*Hope Andrade, former Secretary of State and former Chair of the Texas Transportation Commission.*

"I don't know of any elected official who understands and optimizes every aspect of governing like my friend and colleague, Nelson Wolff. Great lessons in this book."
—*Ricardo A. Samaniego, El Paso County Judge*

"Nelson Wolff's book, *95 Power Principles*, includes lessons learned from decades of public service, lessons essential to success in transforming Bexar County and the city of San Antonio through strategic collaboration and innovation."
—*Patricia E. Roberts, Dean, St. Mary's University School of Law*

"Nelson Wolff hasn't just been a leader, he's gotten big things done. For those of us who served with him, we've seen that work firsthand. Serving both in state government and in local government myself, I know these *95 Power Principles* cannot be ignored. If you believe governing is about getting results, learn these lessons. They have certainly benefited me."
—*Sylvester Turner, Mayor of Houston*

95 POWER PRINCIPLES

Strategies for Effective Leadership in Local Government

Nelson W. Wolff

© 2023 Nelson W. Wolff. All rights reserved. No part of this book may be scanned, copied, uploaded or reproduced in any form or by any means, photographically, electronically or mechanically, without written permission from the copyright holder.

ISBN: 978-1-958407-16-5 (Hardback)
ISBN: 978-1-958407-17-2 (Soft Cover)
ISBN: 978-1-958407-18-9 (eBook)

Book design by designpanache

ELM GROVE PUBLISHING
San Antonio, Texas, USA
www.elmgrovepublishing.com

Elm Grove Publishing is a legally registered trade name of Panache Communication Arts, Inc.

CONTENTS

PREFACE..15
SPECIAL RECOGNITION..17
ACKNOWLEDGEMENTS..18

PATHWAYS TO POWER

1 Establish civic virtue, then test your mettle..........................21
2 Become a sorcerer's apprentice...25
3 Define your turf on a crosstown road map of neighborhoods............27
4 Get your personal life straight before jumping in...................29
5 If the incumbent is teetering on the edge, give a push.............31
6 Apply "Game Theory" in a mayor's race..............................35
7 Finesse an appointment..39

GRASP POWER QUICKLY AND SUSTAIN IT

8 Two for the price of one enhances power............................45
9 Embrace the aura of mayoral power....................................47
10 Generate symbolic acts of purification.................................51
11 Pick an early fight and win...53
12 Act first, create tension, get things done............................55
13 Uncover the hidden and embedded elements of county power........59
14 Crowd out superfluous issues by setting a yearly agenda..........63
15 Get tough on crime..63
16 Establish youth prevention programs...................................69
17 When you have the "Big Mo," double down.........................73
18 Move into vacuums created by vacated power.....................75

19 When facing a major legislative battle procure a cardinal..............77

20 Accumulate, dispense and use information effectively....................81

21 When you lose big, pivot big..85

22 Do not get caught crystal gazing..87

23 When facing a choice between time and money, choose time........89

24 When you don't have the horses, wait them out...............................91

25 A motion to delay is a motion to kill..93

26 Don't let fear of free speech and assembly change who we are........95

27 Don't let process eat you up..99

28 Expect the unexpected...101

ESTABLISH AN EFFECTIVE MANAGEMENT STRUCTURE

29 De-matrix..107

30 Appoint a Thomas Cromwell as your county manager....................109

31 Break up the criminal-industrial complex.......................................113

32 Don't let labor disputes get out of control..117

33 Develop a team of hot and cold lawyers..121

34 Only hire consultants to find a way to your end game...................123

35 Adopt a conservative but flexible budget..125

36 Inspire and take care of your people...127

37 Build a chamber that exemplifies political power..........................129

WORK COLLEAGUES WITH HONEY AND SPICE

38 Take advantage of new colleagues for they know not what they do........135

39 Establish decorum, absorb the hits, and defend your colleagues........137

40 Develop a systematic web of political persuasion with your colleagues....141

41 Develop an underboss..143

42 Squelch groupthink before it leads to mush..145

43 Trade five nickels for a quarter..147

44 Rescue bipartisanship from clans and tribes..149

45 Muffle county-city disputes..153

BUILD COMMUNITY SUPPORT

46 Don't let loose a tsunami of task forces..157

47 Identify and catch the wave of changing power blocs....................159

48 Street smarts are in the streets you know...161

49 Don't punt tough decisions to voters...163

50 Put the kibosh on raising tax rates..165

51 Follow Quintus Tullius Cicero's "rule of yes."................................167

52 Take people to places they resist or never envisioned.....................169

53 Persistence is a close cousin to stubbornness....................................171

54 Tap the power of religious leaders...173

55 Support the small who think big..175

56 Form regional alliances...177

OVERPOWER FRIENDS, ENEMIES, HUSTLERS AND OPPONENTS

57 Don't ride with outlaws...181

58 Use humor to disarm and deflate your critics..................................185

59 Retaliation is best served on a plate of obscurity.............................189

60 Conquer, embrace and assimilate useful opponents.......................193

61 Get another job if you can't work with people you loathe.............195

62 When you clean house expect dust to fall back on the floor..........197

63 Prepare for a landscape covered with bones of broken friendships...199

64 Dance with the devil if he will bring gold to your city.....................203

65 Refuse to dance with sports hustlers, the handmaidens of Beelzebub....205
66 Don't hack off straight-shooting guys who carry suitcases of money.....209
67 Streamline an appointment process...211
68 Beware, the hunter can become the hunted.......................................215
69 Fight the state for local freedom and authority.................................217

COMMUNICATE WITH KNOWLEDGE, TRUTH, AND CLARITY

70 Become an attention merchant...223
71 Dress with sartorial splendor..227
72 Jump on newspaper stories...229
73 Monitor and analyze media coverage...231
74 Buy paid media to highlight major projects.....................................233
75 In a public show down, EI carries the day over IQ..........................235
76 Don't over-react to the "Precautionary Principle."...........................239
77 Know when to shut up..241
78 Rescue truth that is shoved into the abyss of social media..............243
79 Say what you have to say and get out of the way............................247
80 Prepare a monster defense system before you hit the sack..............251
81 Don't smoke and mirror a controversial proposal............................253
82 Stay out of an echo chamber..255
83 Accept no slight of your public office..257

SET THE TABLE TO CREATE SMART JOBS

84 Expand and diversify your economy...261
85 Develop and recruit a skilled workforce...265
86 Embrace creative artists..267
87 Disrupt and innovate to break down barriers to digital information....269

88 Create a tech ecosystem..271
89 Build transforming projects in the urban core......................275
90 Restore, preserve, and enhance fauna and flora...................277
91 Invest in government economic generators.........................281

SET A TIME TO LEAVE
92 Leave at the top of your game...287
93 A long goodbye is best..289
94 Get a new name...291
95 Write to have the last say..293

To my wife Tracy who has been my partner in politics for the last 34 years. She is the love of my life.

PREFACE

Cities and counties touch people's lives in more direct ways than either national or state governments. They are responsible for streets, drainage, public safety, court systems, public hospitals, parks, and thousands of other services.

Smart cities and counties are also incubators for innovation. They foster a creative economic environment by attracting, developing, and retaining entrepreneurial firms and creating a talented work force. Smart cities also support cultural amenities, a vibrant urban lifestyle, clear air, and preserve green space.

San Antonio is one of approximately 20,000 incorporated cities, towns, and villages in the nation. It is the seventh largest city with a population of 1.5 million people.

With two million people, Bexar County is the 19th most populous county in the United States. It includes the city of San Antonio as well as 26 suburban cities and a large unincorporated area.

Mayors and county executives have the opportunity to use their power to significantly change the trajectory of a local community, moving it forward to create a dynamic, prosperous city and county. The change agent for San Antonio was Mayor Henry Cisneros who served as mayor from 1981 to 1989. He changed the role of city government into a powerful proactive engine that led us into a progressive era.

The county judge in Texas is the chair of the five member

Commissioners Court and the chief executive officer of the county. When I became county judge in 2001, I focused on restructuring and streamlining county government and putting it on a path to be a major player with an active role in environmental restoration, therapeutic justice, the arts, sports facilities and health care.

The following principles are derived from my 33 years in government as well as my 36 years of experience as an entrepreneur and CEO. About five years ago, I began writing down principles that I have followed in obtaining, exercising, and enhancing executive power. I eventually came up with 95.* The principles are universal and can be applied in any American city or county.

Under each principle, I have included a short vignette about how the principle was applied in our community. The stories include the actions of other mayors and county executives as well as mine. In most of the episodes, you could substitute players in your own community. I write as if I were speaking directly to a mayor/county executive candidate or officer holder.

The following principles and vignettes will illustrate to the public the attributes of mayoral/county executive leadership necessary to move a community.

---

* There's no magic to that number—but purely by coincidence, Martin Luther listed his *Ninety-five Theses*, a series of observations criticizing the Roman Catholic Church, which he posted on the door of the Wittenberg Castle Church in Germany on October 31, 1517. The *Ninety-five Theses* eventually led to the Reformation of the Church.

SPECIAL RECOGNITION

I had been working on this book for over five years when it finally occurred to me to give Tom Brereton a call. He had worked with me 26 years ago on the book "Mayor" that I wrote in 1997.

I ask him to review a draft that I had written for this book. He called me back and in his blunt way said, "It needs a lot of work."

One must not let your ego get in the way, so I swallowed hard and said, "Maybe you're right."

For the last several months we exchanged drafts back and forth, making changes and checking facts. It is now a much better book because of his input.

Tom graduated from Syracuse University with a doctorate in metropolitan studies and is former professor of urban studies at Trinity University. He is a consultant in planning and urban affairs. He has also been active in local politics since being an advisor to Mayors Henry Cisneros, Howard Peak, Ron Nirenberg and me.

ACKNOWLEDGEMENTS

Let me first thank my wife Tracy for her suggestions. She filled in some gaps and struck out some statements where I was a little too caustic.

I want to thank Dr. Sandi Wolff, my daughter-in-law, who did a superb job of editing this book. It was a huge undertaking on her part and the book is much better because of her.

I thank Bruce Davidson, Communications Director for Mayor Ron Nirenberg, and the former editorial page editor of the *San Antonio Express-News*, for his recommendations.

I appreciate Gilbert Garcia, columnist for *San Antonio Express-News*, for his insight on some the issues.

I thank Mick and Diane Prodger at Elm Grove for publishing for this book, as well as for their insight on the issues I wrote about.

PATHWAYS TO POWER

1

ESTABLISH CIVIC VIRTUE, THEN TEST YOUR METTLE.

You do not wake up one morning and decide you want to be a mayor/county executive without first establishing a political beachhead. Although you may have developed many skills in the private sector as a business or non-profit executive or in academia, it isn't enough for the challenges of obtaining the office of mayor/county executive, nor in providing leadership if you are elected.

In my case, although I had been a state representative and state senator, I had been out of office for 13 years when I set my sights on the office of mayor. I knew I couldn't just come out of nowhere and expect to be elected mayor when practically every sitting City Council member already had similar ambitions.

So, I started by accepting a high profile, non-political role that would give me some public visibility and let me establish a record of demonstrated civic virtue. Mayor Henry Cisneros appointed me chairman of the "Target '90 Commission," an organization established by the San Antonio City Council in 1983 to set goals for the city to achieve by 1990.

I served two one-year terms from 1985 to 1987, during a time that we began to accomplish many of the 93 goals and 353 specific implementation mechanisms. During my chairmanship, we successfully supported a $100 million bond issue that provided funding for several of the goals. We helped defeat a "spending cap" charter amendment that would have hampered achievement of the goals. We also accomplished a significant number of the goals that did not require funding.

Target '90 became a national model. Numerous cities sought information from us about how to establish such an organization. This became the launchpad for my entry into city politics. In 1987, when I completed my second term as chair of the Target '90 Commission, Mayor Cisneros announced that he would be running for his last two-year term. I then decided to run for City Council. If I could be elected to Council and establish a significant record as a council member, I would be in a strong position to run for mayor two years later.

It was no secret to anyone that my intention in running for Council was to use the position as a steppingstone to the mayor's office. There was, however, one small problem. I had to defeat the incumbent councilman, a suburban real estate developer named Ed Harrington, who had the support of the establishment.

Plus, I was a Democrat in a largely Republican district and Harrington was a Republican. Fortunately, San Antonio's municipal elections are non-partisan and the issues of delivering city services do not break along party lines.

Harrington tried to make issues of both my partisan identity when I was in the state legislature and of my obvious mayoral ambitions, but it turned out his constituents didn't care. They knew there are no Democratic or Republican ways of picking up the garbage or filling the potholes. And they knew that if I wanted to be a credible candidate for mayor sometime in the future, I would have to deliver for them first. Then if I were elected mayor two years later, they would have two members on City Council while everyone else in San Antonio had only one.

And so, I took the plunge, knowing that a term on Council would be the best possible preparation for the bigger race. I would be able to establish a record and develop mutually beneficial working relationships with my colleagues. If I lost, I would remain where I belonged, in the pasture of political has-beens looking for another career.

The previous year, in 1986, I had moved into District 8 (one of ten council districts) on the north side of San Antonio. I was thinking ahead by choosing a council district with a large population of well-educated and politically active constituents. It included the sprawling South Texas Medical Center, the University of Texas at San Antonio and the insurance giant USAA, San Antonio's largest employer.

Because Mayor Cisneros had nominal opposition, the *San Antonio Light* newspaper called my race "The Real mayor's race."

I won with 65 percent of the vote and Harrington conceded early on election night. A local magazine carried my picture on its cover and predicted that I would become the next mayor after Cisneros.

Names and times change but principles remain the same. Twenty-six years later in 2013 Ron Nirenberg, a former executive at the Trinity University radio station, ran in the same District 8, letting it be known he wanted to eventually run for mayor. Nirenberg used his civic virtue gained by opposing a proposed Walmart location, thereby establishing himself as a champion of neighborhoods. Although the incumbent councilman did not run for re-election, Nirenberg also had to run against a well-funded candidate. He beat him in a run-off with 54 percent of the vote. He was now positioned to run for mayor.

Show some love and care for your community before you ask for citizens' political support. Best to do something meaningful in a civic venture that will get you visibility. Then run for City Council to establish credibility and learn the ropes.

2

BECOME A SORCERER'S APPRENTICE.

After winning the 1987 council race, I became Mayor Cisneros' shadow, watching him like a wide-eyed hawk. Six years earlier, in 1981 at the age of 33, Cisneros had become the first Hispanic mayor of a large American city.

My "sorcerer" had the charisma to make things happen. He was tall, good-looking, young, charming, persuasive, and dedicated to politics, as powerful as a wizard with supernatural powers, but used for good rather than evil. He was the cat's meow and made San Antonio into a modern city.

Cisneros had a master's degree in city planning from Harvard and a Doctor of Public Administration degree from George Washington University. He served in the local Model Cities administration before successfully running for City Council. He served three two-year terms as councilman, preparing for his successful mayoral race in 1981.

I learned how Cisneros put together a yearly agenda and then created trust and friendship with the council and staff to make it happen. I watched how he used the media to get his message out to the public. I kept notes and hung around after council meetings to talk and spend time with him. I supported his initiatives and eventually became his friend and confidant while preparing myself to succeed him.

I also became acquainted with key players in the bureaucracy who could make things happen. I worked to create a good relationship with other council members. I was able to establish a progressive council record by taking a leadership role on water issues, the public library and recycling.

Not every aspiring mayor will have as clever a sorcerer to follow as I did. Nevertheless, as a councilperson looking ahead, you should carefully observe the mayor to understand his shortcomings and mistakes as well as things he does well.

Likewise, after winning his district race in 2013, District 8 Councilman Ron Nirenberg carefully observed the effective leadership of Mayor Julian Castro, who had created thousands of housing units in the central city through city incentives. When Castro resigned to become Secretary of HUD, Councilwoman Ivy Taylor was appointed to replace him as mayor. Although she was no wizard, Nirenberg made note of her mistakes as well as her successes. He also used his time to learn the ropes of government and establish himself as an environmentalist and advocate for affordable housing.

Studying an incumbent mayor's actions while serving on the council will prepare you for the mayoral race as well as allow you to hit the ground running if you are elected mayor.

3

DEFINE YOUR TURF ON A CROSSTOWN ROAD MAP OF NEIGHBORHOODS.

When I successfully ran for the Texas House and then the Texas Senate, we organized our campaign in the 300 voting precincts in Bexar County. We recruited volunteer leaders who worked with party precinct leaders. They were charged with grassroots campaigning and then getting our supporters to the polls.

Unlike a partisan race, neighborhoods are the key to winning in a non-partisan mayor/council race. Active neighborhood leaders pay attention to what happens at city hall and stay engaged. They are acutely attuned to everything that affects their neighborhood, from zoning and land use to public safety, to animal control, to parks and libraries and streets and sidewalks. In fact, these city issues are more important to them than any of the issues that divide a partisan state legislature or Congress. Therefore, it is critically important to gain their support.

During my 1987 council race, we tapped into the leadership of the neighborhood organizations in my council district. Neighborhood leaders like Bill and Elinor Fries, Dan and Ellie Bump, and Bennie Newman took the lead in organizing neighborhood support in my council race.

After being elected I was the first City Councilman to open a district office and staff it with neighborhood leaders. This put me in sharp contrast to my former opponent, a suburban developer whom neighborhood leaders regarded as one of their natural enemies.

Fries, Bump and Newman were also active in leading the effort to expand the District 8 neighborhood associations into the Northside Neighborhoods for Organized Development. In preparation for the mayor's race we extrapolated our northside neighborhood organization into a citywide neighborhood plan. Our crosstown map highlighted the boundaries of distinct neighborhoods throughout the city including inner city neighborhoods like River Road, Monte Vista, Beacon Hill, Alta Vista, and King William.

Unlike the more affluent northside neighborhoods that are led by secular moderates and conservatives, the inner city neighborhoods are mostly less affluent and led by faith-based coalitions centered around the Catholic church. While we campaigned in those neighborhoods, we chose to target the neighborhoods on the north side that surrounded my council district, and the southeast part of town where I was born and grew up. We block-walked and mailed out several pieces of literature.

Likewise, many years later when District 8 Councilman Ron Nirenberg ran for mayor in 2017, he developed support from a citywide coalition of neighborhoods. He also expanded his network of environmentalists who were also active in neighborhoods. He now had a roadmap to victory in his future mayoral race.

Without the support of neighborhood leaders in your mayoral campaign you will probably end up as burnt toast. So, get to know neighborhood leaders and commit to the issues that will make their neighborhoods better.

4

GET YOUR PERSONAL LIFE STRAIGHT BEFORE JUMPING IN.

There was a time when your private life was separated from your political life. Not so anymore. In a high-profile mayoral race, you can expect that every aspect of your personal life will be scrutinized.

On September 12, 1988, Henry Cisneros announced that he would not run for another term, and I jumped into the race to succeed him. But I had a little problem. I had gone through an uncontested divorce, but the property settlement, which was more than a few bucks, was not final. Moreover, I was already falling in love with a wonderful woman.

Two agonizing months after announcing my candidacy, I decided it was time to seek the advice of my sorcerer who had been through a conflicted love for another woman. In early November 1988, I had breakfast with Mayor Cisneros at the Holiday Inn on Loop 410. I told him I was falling in love with a woman and that we had decided to not reveal our love until after the mayor's race.

Henry said, "I have been so bonded to politics that I feel like I am made of wire and plastic and metal instead of flesh and blood.

If you love someone, get out of the race. If you do not, the media will follow every move you make and speculate about your personal relationship. The price is not worth an unhappy personal life."

Henry was right; I finally realized that the price of higher political office was above my southside price limit. So, I chose love over politics, knowing that I had given up my great ambition to become mayor. I called a press conference on November 9, 1988, and withdrew from the race.

On January 1, 1989, I married the love of my life, Tracy. I ran for re-election to the City Council winning with 80 percent of the vote in the May election.

Former Mayor Lila Cockrell, who had preceded Cisneros as mayor, came back and easily won the mayoral race.

Scrub, polish and get your personal life in order before announcing for office.

5

IF THE INCUMBENT IS TEETERING ON THE EDGE, GIVE A PUSH.

Lila Cockrell had been the perfect mayor (1975-81) during a turbulent time of transition from a council elected at-large to one elected from single member districts that were forced upon the city under the Voting Rights Act in 1977. Single member districts empowered the city's "minority-majority" for the first time. The newly-empowered minority-majority aggressively asserted its authority leading to conflicts with the Anglo minority councilmembers.

Cockrell offered no substantial agenda of her own, but she did an outstanding job guiding the city through the difficult transition to an ethnically diverse political system. But this wasn't what San Antonio needed at the cusp of the 1990s, after eight years of dynamism under Henry Cisneros.

At our first council meeting in June 1987 as expected, she did not lay out her agenda. Instead, advisory committees, whom she had appointed before she took office, reported back to her. One of these was on the city budget and fiscal policy.

The city had a history of depending on economic growth and one-time revenues to cover budget expenses. But we were now facing an economic slowdown. Property values were declining, and unemployment had risen to 7.9 percent.

Cockrell's budget committee recommended several good changes to the budget process. They also recommended an increase in property taxes by 22 to 34 percent.

After delaying her decision for several months, Cockrell supported a tax increase of 12 percent that was recommended by the city manager. The City Council, including me, voted 9-2 to increase taxes by 12 percent.

Around the same time, it also became public that the recently approved police union contract would cost several times the amount City Council had been told and that the budget office had been excluded from the negotiations.

Councilmen Jimmy Hasslocher, Weir Labatt and I met with Mayor Cockrell and asked her to seek City Manager Lou Fox's resignation. She decided not to.

Citizens were enraged and gathered petitions to overturn the tax increase. As a result, her mayor-mobile started skidding around on the slick streets of San Antonio, sliding toward the edge of a cliff.

Then on January 26, 1990, only a week before the tax "rollback" election day, Cockrell blamed former Mayor Cisneros for spending too much. The break with Henry clearly measured her desperation in a losing battle. Voters overturned the tax increase with 65 percent of the vote.

With all her missteps she was now teetering on the edge of a cliff. I decided a little push would do the trick. I jumped in and announced my candidacy.

Although she was vulnerable, she still had an extraordinary advantage with name recognition and in holding onto almost all high-profile community leaders. But in a highly visible race, endorsements have little influence. Voters will make up their own mind.

But you must have the bucks to overcome the mayor's establishment support. I committed $300,000 of my own money and got commitments of $700,000 more, mostly from my former business associates.

Unfortunately, I was not the only one to notice her vulnerability. Two of my council colleagues, a former councilman, a community activist and five other candidates eventually entered the race. I now had a much more significant challenge than I would have had if I had stayed in the mayoral race a year before.

Many years later, in 2016 Councilman Ron Nirenberg also noticed Mayor Ivy Taylor teetering on the edge. She had voted against a non-discrimination ordinance. She then later got into a fight over a river barge contract with popular City Manager Sheryl Sculley and former Mayor Phil Hardberger. Seeing her clinging to the edge, Nirenberg announced he would run against Mayor Taylor in the 2017 election.

If you want to be the Man, do not be afraid to take on the incumbent and the establishment.

6

APPLY "GAME THEORY" IN A MAYOR'S RACE.

John Forbes Nash, Jr.'s 28-page paper on "game theory" deals with strategic behavior in non-cooperative games. The assumption is that everyone playing has equal knowledge and will act in a reasonable manner. Even though everyone is capable of sharing common knowledge, a winner has to better process it and make it into more complete knowledge than the other players.

Game theory can be applied successfully in any zero-sum game, including a mayor's race. In 1990 I had to develop a sophisticated implementation of game theory to overcome the advantages of an incumbent mayor and the other nine candidates in the race.

You must have the ability to decipher information, looking for the issues voters will respond to and then act on that information. You also need to be able to assimilate knowledge of your opponents and anticipate their reaction to whatever action you may take.

Our poll showed that Mayor Cockrell had a 59 percent voter approval rating and would beat me 50 percent to 30 percent. But it also showed that two-thirds of the voters would support new leadership in the mayor's office if they had a new vision for the city. That information revealed that it was a winnable race if I could show voters I could provide the leadership they were looking for.

On September 18, 1990, we had our campaign kickoff. I pledged to develop a new agenda to carry San Antonio through the 1990s. I outlined three major themes: better jobs, safer neighborhoods, and quality education.

Our neighborhood leaders had organized a political action committee called "Neighborhoods Now!" and endorsed me in the race for mayor. They formed the "Wolff Pack" and developed a specially designed bandana to wear to all political events. They became the core support of my campaign.

While we accentuated the positive, we also had to convince voters that mayor Cockrell should not be re-elected. Voters remember at most two or three things about a candidate when they cast their ballots. Human nature being what it is, voters are more likely to remember the negative than the positive.

So based on Mayor Cockrell's personality, I knew she was sensitive to criticism and the odds were that she would overreact if I attacked her record. If she did counterattack, I would separate from the pack of the other nine challengers.

We began with a news conference on January 29. Lila's leadership style was outdated, I charged. I said she was only "window dressing" and "ribbon cutting."

She said she was "shocked, angry, and disgusted," charging that my attacks revealed "a desperate candidate with a badly faltering campaign."

We then ran a television ad questioning her leadership and she struck back with a negative television spot against me. I was now seen as her greatest threat to re-election. We kept up the pressure by continuing our criticism.

We then produced a television ad alleging a conflict of interest that the mayor had with Valero Energy CEO Bill Greehey, who was her campaign finance chair. His firm had a contract with City Public Service (now CPS Energy), the city owned utility that Cockrell was an *ex officio* board member of. We made sure he got a copy of our television spot.

I knew Greehey was a tough, strong CEO who would not tolerate political punches. He would strike back. Sure enough he did. He sent a letter to his employees asking them to vote against me. We obtained a copy of the letter and gave it to the media.

I was now clearly identified as an independent candidate who was not afraid to stand up to big business and the establishment. I had separated myself from the pack. By the way, we never ran that television spot.

I was able to read both the mayor and Greehey correctly, acted on my assessment of their personalities, and got the response I expected. It was so well planned that we knocked the mayor out of the runoff. The results were that Councilmember María Berriozabál, who had succeeded Cisneros representing District 1, led the first-round vote with 30.5 percent. I had 26.157 percent and Mayor Cockrell had 20.68 percent.

Based on successfully processing our knowledge we had also ignored all the other candidates in the race, including Berriozabal. Now that we were in a runoff with her we deployed the same strategy. We ran a positive campaign pounding away at the need for effective leadership. We got our vote out and won the runoff election.

In 2017 Ron Nirenberg also deployed "game theory" effectively in his race against Mayor Ivy Taylor. He was hoping to be in a heads-up race, but Manuel Medina, chair of the local Democratic Party, entered the race.

Instead of taking the mayor out like I did, Nirenberg's

"game theory" was to take Medina out and then garner his Hispanic support in a runoff against Mayor Taylor. He nailed Medina by revealing that he had run for political office in Mexico and criticizing him for running political campaigns in Panama.

It was a smart move. He eliminated Medina from the runoff. With Medina knocked out he consolidated his Hispanic support. In the runoff he convinced Taylor to have over 30 debates. Debates almost always inure to the benefit of challengers. Nirenberg was a better debater and got under her skin.

Like Mayor Cockrell in my race, Mayor Taylor overreacted and ran negative ads against Nirenberg, calling him an out of touch liberal. Nirenberg won the runoff with 54 percent of the vote.

Implement "game theory" by better processing knowledge into a more complete understanding than the other players. And then act on that knowledge in an aggressive manner, taking calculated risks to win the race.

7

FINESSE AN APPOINTMENT.

On occasions, an opportunity to be appointed mayor/county executive may arise when an incumbent dies or decides to resign during their term of office. Five years after being term-limited out as mayor in 1995, such an opportunity came my way.

At the same time, as CEO of our nine Sun Harvest Natural Food Supermarket stores, I had concluded the sale of our company to Wild Oats Natural Foods, a national chain, in early 2000.

Republican County Judge Cyndi Krier, the county's chief executive officer and chair of the Commissioners Court (the county's legislative body), had previously said she would only serve two terms and that precluded a re-election campaign in 2002. I let it be known that I would run for County Judge in the 2002 election cycle.

I now had to transition from a non-partisan city election to a partisan county election. I would first have to run in the Democratic party primary and then the general election. By the summer of 2000, my proposed candidacy began to gain legs as word of mouth spread. Word of mouth is uncontrollable and fickle, but when it works right, it is the most powerful form of politics. And it was working for me.

Instead of finishing her term, Judge Krier announced that she would resign to become a member of the Board of Regents of the University of Texas System. The Commissioners Court would appoint her successor. In recent history, three Bexar County Judges had resigned and in all three instances, the court picked one of their colleagues on the court. History did not speak well for my chances. I first met with Judge Krier and she said she would consider me, even though I was a Democrat.

I then met with Commissioner Tommy Adkisson. Bad news, he wanted the job. So, I enlisted the help of my great late friend, prominent trial lawyer Pat Maloney, who put the pressure on Tommy and eventually Tommy came on board to support me.

On October 22, I attended a fundraiser for Commissioner Robert Tejeda and asked for his support. He said he would consider me.

In February 2001 over a plate of enchiladas, Commissioner Paul Elizondo, the senior member of the court, said "I was interested in the appointment, but Cyndi would not support me. You did a good job as mayor. So, I will support you."

Paul then put the pressure on Tejeda and brought him on board.

I then met with Republican Commissioner Lyle Larson, who served on the council when I was mayor. He was an independent minded Republican and told me, "I would rather vote for a good Democrat than have a bad Republican jammed down my throat."

On April 24, 2001, the Commissioners Court voted unanimously to appoint me as County Judge pending the Senate confirmation of Krier's appointment. The following day the Texas Senate confirmed Krier, and I took the oath of County Judge. I ran for election the following year and won easily.

Many years later in May 2014, Councilperson Ivy Taylor saw an opportunity to be appointed mayor. Mayor Julian Castro had accepted an appointment to serve as secretary of HUD in President Barack Obama's cabinet.

While several councilmen jockeyed for the appointment, including Ron Nirenberg, she was able to get the support of respected northside Councilman Joe Krier (Cyndi's husband) who then teamed up with southside councilmember Rebecca Viagran to get a council majority.

Krier and Viagran had a persuasive argument that Taylor would become the first African American mayor of San Antonio. Taylor positioned herself as a safe choice by promising not to run for election for a full term. She was chosen by the City Council on July 22, 2014.

She did not keep her promise and successfully ran for mayor in 2015, only to face Nirenberg again in 2017.

When seeking to be appointed to office, develop a strategy to work the council/commissioner members. That means understanding their personalities, meeting with them to assure them that you will support their initiatives and enlisting their supporters to put pressure on them to appoint you.

GRASP POWER QUICKLY AND SUSTAIN IT

8

TWO FOR THE PRICE OF ONE ENHANCES POWER.

When I was elected mayor, I said the public was getting two for the price of one, meaning my wife Tracy would be a power in herself.

We came together as two strong individuals following the tenets of Kahlil Gibran's poem *The Prophet:*

> *Stand together yet not too near together*
> *For the pillars of the temple stand apart,*
> *And the oak tree and the cypress grow not in each other's shadow.*

Tracy was a former executive for Texas A&M Extension Service and Target '90, and had overseen my mayoral campaign. A striking blond standing 5'9", weighing 120 lbs. with a 24-inch waist, she made heads turn. Beneath her beauty was inner strength that surfaced when someone crossed her or me.

During my term as mayor, she carved out her agenda that included children as her priority. She co-founded "Smart Start" to raise money to support childcare. She raised millions of dollars for the San Antonio library and the downtown Children's Museum.

She set a tone of "Camelot" in our city by creating a social scene that highlighted arts, culture, and fashion. She hosted the initialing of the NAFTA agreement in San Antonio by President George H. Bush, Mexican President Carlos Salinas and Canadian Prime Minister Brian Mulroney. During an international conference she organized a state dinner on the stage of the Majestic Theater for President George Bush and the presidents of six Latin American countries. She also hosted a lunch for Barbara Bush attended by a cross section of 300 leading women. She was greeted with awe on our Asian trips to Japan, Taiwan, and Hong Kong.

When I became county judge in 2001, she founded the Hidalgo Foundation and raised millions of dollars to fund the building of a new children's court, the restoration of our historic courthouse, and to develop BibilioTech, the county's all digital libraries.

We supported each other but did not interfere with each other's agenda with the understanding that the oak tree and the cypress grow not in each other's shadow.

Other San Antonio mayors and county judges' spouses have also been effective partners. Judge Cyndi Krier's (1991-2001) husband Joe was president of the Greater San Antonio Chamber of Commerce and would later (2013-2017) become a San Antonio City Councilman.

During Mayor Phil Hardberger's term (2005-09) his wife Linda led the effort to build pocket parks throughout the city. Mayor Ron Nirenberg's (2017-2025) wife, Erika Prosper, was chair of the Hispanic Chamber and led the effort to promote equity in city funding.

If you have a spouse, tap into their strength. Encourage them to develop their own agenda, then support them, and bask in the power they will bring to you.

9

EMBRACE THE AURA OF MAYORAL POWER.

The prestigious title of "mayor" is one of the most highly valued laurels of political status. However, a title is just a title and nothing more unless you are willing to embrace the mayoral aura of power and be a leader.

In a "strong mayor" form of government, power is embedded in the office, giving the mayor power to hire his own management team. In a council-manager form of government, the City Council hires the city manager who reports to the council instead of the mayor. The city staff works for the city manager, not the mayor. Embracing mayoral power and exercising it is harder in a council-manager form of city government.

San Antonio has had a council-manager system since 1952. At that same time the Good Government League (GGL) was founded. In closed door meetings they selected the nine candidates for City Council who then selected the mayor from among themselves. They chose candidates who were committed to having council act as a board of directors and let the city managers run the city. They held power for over 20 years, winning 77 out of 81 at-large council seats. They finally lost their power in 1973, when their council majority unexpectedly split and elected Charles Becker mayor instead of their intended candidate. Two years later voters approved the direct election of the mayor and elected Lila Cockrell, who had previously been a GGL Councilmember. But even after 10 single member districts replaced the all at-large Council in 1977, the mayor still acted as a chairman of the board of directors of a business instead of assuming responsibility as the top elected official of city government. The city managers dominated mayors, setting policy and priorities rather than acting as a Chief Operating Officer.

That changed in 1981 when Henry Cisneros became the first mayor to embrace the aura of power. To overcome the inherent lack of mayoral structural power, he knew how to count to six (the majority of the council). He quickly put together council votes to fire city manager Tom Huebner, who had a drinking problem, and hire his assistant Lou Fox in his place. Fox got it. For eight years, Cisneros enacted policies and established priorities and City Manager Fox acted as the Chief Operating Officer, carrying out his initiatives.

In Cisneros, the people of San Antonio finally had an effective mayor who addressed numerous issues that unelected city managers had previously ignored. For the first time, minorities were elevated to an equal status with the Anglo race. Inner city street and drainage projects, parks, a new central library, and literacy centers were built.

When I was a councilman, I had supported Alex Briseño when we appointed him city manager to succeed Lou Fox, so we had a relationship before I became mayor. When I became mayor in 1991, we reached an agreement that I would support all his management decisions and he would support my major initiatives.

During my two terms as mayor, Briseño quickly recognized that I knew how to count to six and could always put my votes together. When I proposed a major project I would ask, "I am going across the street. Are you with me?" He always said yes. Without his loyalty and support, we would not have accomplished many of the major initiatives we undertook.

However, over the years since I left office, mayoral leadership has been spotty. Some mayors stood up and led, others deferred to the city manager (*More on this story is in Principle 30*).

A mayor must have a clear understanding with the city manager that the manager is the chief operating officer and not the leader of the city. Let them know that you know how to count and that you will have the votes on the council to enact the policies you have set out.

10

GENERATE SYMBOLIC ACTS OF PURIFICATION.

Symbolic acts of purification after winning a mayoral race provide a cleansing from the hard scrabble of a contentious political campaign. Through acts of purification, you become associated with righteousness that sets the stage for healing, enabling you to quickly exercise political power.

On the morning after our mayoral victory in May 1991, Archbishop Patrick Flores gave Tracy and me his blessing at a worship ceremony held at St. Peter and St. Joseph's Children's Home. With a city that is predominantly Hispanic and Catholic, it was a powerful purification message following a contentious mayoral race.

A few days later, I chose the historic Arneson River Theater, located at a bend of the downtown river, to hold our swearing-in ceremony. I arrived, along with the City Council, on a river barge to the music of the Mercado Mariachis band.

After the swearing-in, I gave a speech saying that the political battle was over, and it was time to mend fences and act together regardless of whom anybody supported in the mayoral race. Afterwards the Citywide Revival Choir sang several gospel songs.

Later in the day, Tracy and I attended worship services at

Antioch Baptist church and then New Light Baptist church on the east side, home to the majority of African Americans in San Antonio. I promised them that they would be at the table of "equity and decision."

In 2005 after Phil Hardberger defeated Julian Castro, he reached out to COPS/Metro, a major Hispanic organization, and offered his support on several issues. He was sworn in at the Institute of Texan Cultures, a symbol of inclusion.

In 2017, when Ron Nirenberg defeated Ivy Taylor, he was sworn in on the same Arneson River Theater stage as I was. Having defeated an African American female mayor, he also reached out to the Black churches.

After winning, open your arms like a preacher man on Sunday mornings. Gather in your new flock, embrace them, and show your love in a visible way. Healing leads to leading.

11

PICK AN EARLY FIGHT AND WIN.

Winning the first battle is like scoring the first touchdown in a football game. The first to score is likely the winner. The office of the mayor or county executive is about winning and there is no better way to win than to score on the first play and show the community who is boss.

When picking that first fight, make them come to your turf. Right after I was elected mayor, I convened a meeting with the board members of the Workforce Commission (our local job training agency) in my conference room and asked them all to resign. Many of them had conflicts of interest as they worked behind the scenes to acquire contracts for themselves or agencies they worked for.

Although I did not have the authority to remove them, almost all of them thought that I did and resigned that same day. *San Antonio Light* columnist Rick Casey said he had not seen power exercised like this since the early days of Henry Cisneros.

After becoming county judge in 2001, I picked a fight with the county constables whose offices are relics of the 1876 Texas constitution. County sheriffs could and should perform all the duties of constables were it not for the state constitution. Over strong objections, I won the battle to eliminate one of the five Bexar County constables (four were protected by the state constitution). It saved the county some $1 million a year.

After Phil Hardberger won his race for mayor in 2005, he quickly moved to appoint Sheryl Sculley city manager and Michael Bernard city attorney. The City Council approved both appointments setting the stage for his successful two terms.

Picking an early fight and winning sets the stage for prevailing in later battles. It puts everyone on notice that you will exercise your power.

12

ACT FIRST, CREATE TENSION, GET THINGS DONE.

After picking an early fight and winning, you have now become a wolf among the hounds. Wolves have strong jaws, sharp teeth, great instincts, and attack with vigor. When new political fights emerge, bite first like a wolf, stick it out there with an aggressive first action, and put all your political opponents on their heels searching for a tree to climb. Once your foe is up on the tree don't let up. Keep him there.

I learned to be aggressive from playing no-limit table stakes Hold'em poker. There is no way to win playing a conservative, calling game. You must take calculated risks and bet, bet, bet, putting the pressure on your opponents, making them lay down winning hands. The same strategy applies to politics.

While your opposition is stricken with analysis/paralysis trying to figure how to react, you are off and running, increasing the strength of your political winds, and gaining support. You can win the battle even if you hold a weaker hand because your opponent may fold his hand for fear of your first move.

As you enter a battle, tension will build as the fight gets underway. Creating tension is much like tightening violin strings. You string them tight as you can, hoping the strings do not break. That is good because it will heighten your senses and energy as you sustain the tension to get things done like moving controversial projects forward. When facing adversity, you will learn more about yourself. Do you have it in you to sustain your stamina over a long period of time?

In 1999, the San Antonio Spurs were playing in the city-owned Alamodome – a facility designed for football, not basketball. They wanted a new arena to be financed by the hotel-motel and car rental taxes because they would be paid primarily by out-of-town visitors and be easier to get voter approval for rather than a sales tax. Mayor Howard Peak took the lead in opposing use the hotel-motel tax because he wanted the funds reserved for the city to use for convention related business.

County Judge Cyndi Krier strung the strings tight when she acted fast and supported a hotel-motel and car rental tax to build a new arena for the Spurs. The county had never initiated a major project, so the city did not take them seriously.

Krier convinced voters to approve the hotel-motel tax and to build the arena on county land three miles east of downtown. This was the first major victory for the county by Krier's quick action.

In 2005, Mayor Phil Hardberger acted first and fast to re-design and enlarge the historic Main Plaza by proposing to close the four streets surrounding it. The downtown merchants, who opposed closing any of the streets, were caught off guard.

Hardberger softened their opposition by agreeing to only close two of the streets and then quickly got council approval. The restored and enlarged plaza now provides a beautiful framing of San Fernando Cathedral and connects it to the San Antonio River entrance that was built during Mayor Howard Peak's two terms (1997-2001).

In November 2012, Mayor Julian Castro created the first

city run pre-K program by acting quickly to pass a sales tax before the school superintendents and anti-tax folks could organize to beat him. Since opening the pre-K schools, they have served 8,000 students in four quality education centers that City Manager Sheryl Sculley spearheaded.

In 2013, as county judge I acted fast to build the nation's first digital public library before the supporters of the city library system could organize opposition. The city library system, which the county financially supported, was not addressing the need for digital access by people in low- income areas. They were also not providing adequate services to the 500,000 county citizens outside the city limits.

We kept our plans secret until we began construction. We then fast paced the construction and opened within a few months *(Story in Principle 87)*.

Although you will lose sometimes by being first, you win nothing riding in the caboose and reacting to others. If you act second and go along with someone else's initiative and it is a failure you will be held accountable. If it prevails, you will get no credit.

We found that to be true in 2010 when the city took the lead in putting together an incentive package to entice Incube, a California biotech company, to relocate three of their divisions to San Antonio. The city put up $6 million, two other investors put up $2 million and I made the mistake of supporting a county investment of $2 million even though I had reservations. They said they would create at least 50 high paying jobs but only created eight. It was a very bad investment, and it was a failure on my part when I followed the city's lead.

Following is a recipe for passivity and will lead to failure of leadership. Be aggressive, bite first, stick it out there and put your opponents on the defensive.

13

UNCOVER THE HIDDEN AND EMBEDDED ELEMENTS OF COUNTY POWER.

While the mayor is bestowed with aura and prestige, county executives are largely invisible in major metropolitan areas. The mayor is the big cheese in town while the county executive has limited power and visibility. In Texas, county executives are called the County Judge, which makes it even more confusing.

The 1876 Texas state constitution created a fragmented county government that divides power among separately elected officials alongside the "Commissioners Court" which is the county legislative body. These include an elected county clerk, district clerk (for the court system), tax assessor-collector, district attorney, sheriff, and countless black-robed judges. The county has no power beyond what the state constitution and legislature explicitly give it – and that is not much.

Judge Cyndi Krier had taken an extraordinary step when she convinced voters to use the hotel-motel tax as the way to pay for the new county arena. When I became county judge in 2001, it was my job along with the Commissioners Court and staff to oversee the construction of the arena.

Other than Krier's leadership on the arena, I was dismayed to find out how weak and irrelevant Bexar County really was. I publicly labeled county government as "weird" and out of date and said it had been "largely relegated to the backwaters of urban government."

It took me several years to uncover every fragment of power hidden within the labyrinth of county government. I first learned to use the budget as a heavy hammer to bring other elected officials into line. It is a very blunt instrument for influencing their policies.

I also researched state statutes, finding power hidden in complicated legislation. That is where I found the power to use hotel-motel taxes for various projects that stretched the limits of its purpose (to benefit the visitor industry) beyond professional sports venues and convention facilities. *(More on this in Principle 33).*

For most of my term I successfully lobbied the Texas Legislature for additional authority, such as the public improvement district authority that had expanded authority to tax and regulate development along with environmental safeguards. We used that authority to develop a resort hotel and PGA golf courses. *(You will find more on that story in Principle 19).*

Since I became county judge, we created an economic development department, a public information office, a criminal justice planning department, a public defender office, an environmental office, a digital public library, an independent election administrator office, and established emergency service districts in the unincorporated area.

Increasing the power of county government has enabled Bexar County to become an effective voice in our community. But it was a long battle over the first ten years of my almost 22-year term.

County power lurks in dark corners. It's up to you to stick around long enough to find it, enhance it, and use it.

14

CROWD OUT SUPERFLUOUS ISSUES BY SETTING A YEARLY AGENDA.

A yearly agenda keeps everyone focused and makes it difficult for any member to later add superfluous items. Cisneros was the first mayor to set an agenda and I noticed it.

On the opening day of my first council session as mayor in 1991, I laid out a one-year agenda consisting of 37 specific objectives to be achieved. I included other council members' ideas along with mine. One will always fight harder for one's own ideas. I mentioned each colleague by name as taking the lead on at least one of the items. By doing so in effect I drafted them onto my team. With a joint declaration through a yearly agenda, we had to work together to be successful.

The agenda included developing a new job training program, implementing a citywide recycling program, establishing new scenic corridors, passing a restrictive sign ordinance, and holding taxes to the rate of inflation.

I kept a list on my desk and one in my shirt pocket and would check them off as the year proceeded. It makes for a good report card.

Years later, as county executive at my first meeting on May 8, 2001, I laid out an agenda that included building the county arena where the Spurs would play, establishing an independent election administrator, hosting a health care summit, and restoring the courthouse to its historic grandeur.

I promoted my county agenda using my two annual State of the County speeches, held by the Greater San Antonio Chamber of Commerce and the North San Antonio Chamber of Commerce. Speaking before a combined audience of over 1,000 people, I had the opportunity to garner public support for major projects. By gaining public support, it also put pressure on the commissioners to support the agenda.

You can't bake a cake without the right ingredients. So, cook up a tasty cake with enticing ingredients and promote your agenda with your councilperson/commissioners and citizens.

15

GET TOUGH ON CRIME.

When I was mayor in the 1990s the city was facing a major crime wave, with a record number of homicides. Police Chief Bill Gibson and I announced at a press conference the formation of a 102-member violent crimes task force backed by a 141-member investigative task force. They would concentrate on high crime areas of the city in the hours when most crime was committed.

Within a few months police recorded 840 felony arrests with the seizure of 295 weapons and 5,000 rounds of ammunition and the murder rate began to fall. By the end of my two terms as mayor, violent crime dropped 45 percent and overall crime by approximately 30 percent. Getting tough on crime worked.

At the same time, I created a 29-member Crime Prevention Commission, chaired by Councilman Lyle Larson, to come up with a plan to get citizens involved fighting crime. Based on their recommendations, we created a Cellular on Patrol program providing civilians with cell phones and training to report suspicious activities. We started a Citizen Police Academy to teach people how to implement prevention programs. We created downtown foot and bike patrols, a domestic violence unit, and foot patrols in housing projects. We opened more police substations that included community meeting rooms where a working relationship between the police and neighborhood leaders developed.

To stop criminals and youth gangs from getting guns I banned gun shows at city facilities, passed a weapons ordinance, levied a fine for discharging a gun within the city, prohibited persons 17 and younger from carrying guns in public, and called on parents to search their children's rooms for guns and turn them in if they wished. My office was flooded with angry calls, but it worked, and gun violence subsided.

Over the years since I was mayor the National Rifle Association has grown stronger. Since 2020, over 60 million guns have been sold in the United States. Researchers repeatedly found that a gun in the home makes people more likely to be murdered, not less.

The leading cause of death in the United States for children and teenagers is now gun violence. More than 4,300 young people died from gun violence in the 2020. Two cheerleaders were shot in April 2023 in an Austin HEB supermarket parking lot after one approached the wrong car. They were both seriously injured. The list of shootings goes on.

By 2022, gun deaths increased in Texas as state leaders led by Governor Greg Abbott weakened control of guns and even promoted them. In the seven years since Governor Abbot was elected in 2015, children have become more than twice as likely to die from gun violence.

In the last 14 years Texas has had nine mass shootings. It has led the nation since 2018 in mass shooting and gun deaths.

After the mass shooting of 19 children and two teachers on May 24, 2022, at Robb Elementary School in Uvalde, Texas, only 90 miles from San Antonio, it seemed people were finally ready for change.

Ten days later, I called a press conference along with Sheriff Javier Salazar, District Attorney Joe Gonzalez, and leaders of "Mothers Demand Action." We asked Governor Abbott to call a special session to take up gun control that would include raising the age from 18 to 21 to buy semi-automatic weapons, enacting a Red Flag law, requiring training to obtain a license to carry firearms, requiring background checks on all gun sales and state funding for school security upgrades and trauma emergency planning.

Of course, Abbott did not call one. Instead, in an unbelievable move, Governor Abbott in April 2023 announced just a few hours after Daniel Perry was convicted of killing an armed "Black Lives Matter" protester in Austin that he would pardon him as soon as he could. Under Texas law they could both carry guns. After it became public that Perry had written before the shooting that he wanted to kill protesters, Muslims and Blacks, Abbott began to squirm.

In 2023 legislature session legislators still refused to address reasonable gun control.

Work with your police chief to target serious crime, enlist citizen help, and have the guts to stand up to the NRA.

16

ESTABLISH YOUTH PREVENTION PROGRAMS.

While we took a hard line against serious crimes when I was mayor, we also established programs to offer opportunities for youths to have a safe haven away from gangs. We launched "Operation Cool" at 35 sites for Night Owl recreation programs, and we extended swimming pool hours. In a partnership with the private sector, we started the "Coalition." Slogans such as "Improve your hang time," and "Join the Co" encouraged young people to sign up for numerous programs that the private sector funded. More than 30,000 young people signed up.

We also created a Youth Commission of 22 students in grades 10 through 12. They made suggestions to the City Council regarding the youth programs we should fund. By the way, the Youth Commission still exists today.

As result of their recommendations, we increased the city budget for youth programs from $10 million to $50 million. They also helped us implement a youth curfew that would remain in effect until youth violence was under control.

We also began an after-school care program, starting with 20 schools and expanding to 60 schools before I left office. Kids could stay at school until 5:30 p.m., giving parents extra time to pick up their youngsters after work.

We won three national awards for our youth programs. Prevention programs worked as youth crime decreased.

Many years later in 2014 as County Judge, I teamed up with Mayor Julian Castro to create a city/county commission, chaired by Councilman Rey Saldaña, to address the broken juvenile truancy system. Too many parents were charged with criminal acts because their children skipped school. As many as 32,000 criminal cases were filed each year, causing havoc with families.

In response to the commission's report, we convinced the legislature to decriminalize truancy. School districts agreed to institute early intervention programs to help students and parents before they accumulated too many absences. As a result of our efforts truancy dropped from 32,000 to 16,000.

In 2003, my wife Tracy raised $3 million to build a 10,000 sq. ft. state of the art children's court. It included the latest in technology, provided ample room for families, social service agencies, Child Protective Services, defense attorneys, prosecutors and a special room for children equipped with children's furniture and books and games.

Tracy partnered with Judge John Specia and Judge Peter Sakai to create an early intervention court to help stabilize families before their children were removed from them. Along with funds raised by Tracy the Commissioners Court also funded a family drug court that coordinated health services to parents who were addicted to drugs. We provided wraparound services to help families become stable and keep their children.

I convinced the Commissioners Court to create a pretrial diversion program for first time youth offenders. More than 770 youths were placed in the program. Other juveniles were put on probation and overseen by a staff trained in motivational interviewing skills, trauma care, and services that include aggression replacement training, family therapy, and cognitive services.

Show a little love to youth by listening to them, creating outreach programs that include recreational and educational programs, and a safe environment. Reach out to troubled families to help stabilize a good environment for their children.

17

WHEN YOU HAVE THE "BIG MO," DOUBLE DOWN.

When an athlete is on a streak, he begins to play over his head. He feels invincible, gaining greater confidence as he extends his streak. For a length of time, he simply cannot be beaten. So, like an athlete, swing away when you have the "Big Mo."

When the odds are even on any given bet, the odds of winning three consecutive times are 8-1 against you. However, when you have the Big Mo, you can overcome the odds.

In the late 1980s Mayor Cisneros had the Big Mo when he won four big voter approved issues in a row. Cisneros won tax increases to pay for street and drainage projects, to build a new central library, and to build the Alamodome. He also turned back an effort to amend the city charter to impose a "spending cap" on the city budget.

In 1995 after serving as mayor, I took over as the CEO of Sun Harvest Natural Food Supermarkets. Using my experience as mayor, I doubled down, got the Big Mo and within three years, I built and opened three successful new stores in a row.

In 2005-2009 former Mayor Hardberger also had the Big Mo by winning three times in a row. He gained support for the restoration and expansion of Main Plaza, extending the San Antonio Riverwalk north, and increasing council term limits from two 2-year terms to four 2-year terms. *(More about each of these issues in other principles).*

I thought that I had the Big Mo in 2008 when voters approved a $414 million bond issue and then two months later the Commissioners Court passed a tax increase to pay for a new $900 million county hospital and clinical building. However, I lost my third big issue, when I failed to obtain a downtown site for a new baseball stadium. I still had a .666 batting average, and I will take that.

Press when you have the momentum. Go for multiple scores when you have a hot hand. When it gives way and it will, take your loss, then pause, take a breath, and prepare for the next round of battles hoping that you will catch the next Big Mo.

18

MOVE INTO VACUUMS CREATED BY VACATED POWER.

In 2002, Mayor Ed Garza initially did not support pursuing a Toyota pickup truck manufacturing plant. He wrote, "I'm picturing dirty industrial buildings, tall smokestacks, and thick black fumes. I am not only skeptical but angry about the Toyota proposal." Adding to his hesitancy, the city was further compromised when two City Council members were indicted on October 9, 2002, for taking bribes.

At the time San Antonio had very few manufacturing jobs. In fact, the last time a vehicle assembly plant was located in Texas was 50 years in the past. I thought if we landed the plant, we could eventually transform our economy by attracting more manufacturing firms that pay wages 17 percent higher than other jobs.

So, I stepped in as county judge to fill the vacuum and led a team to attract Toyota. I began meeting several times a week with Toyota executive Dennis Cueno, who was in charge of deciding which city they would locate in. I led the effort to negotiate a tax abatement plan, provided infrastructure funding, negotiated the dual rail service they required and successfully lobbied the legislature to provide financial incentives for both the Toyota plant and its 23 mostly manufacturing suppliers that would be located right next door.

Finally, Mayor Garza changed his mind and became supportive of Toyota. Eventually Toyota chose San Antonio. They built a state-of-the art manufacturing plant that is virtually pollution free. As of 2022, over 8,000 employees are working for Toyota and their current 26 suppliers.

Since then, we have attracted many other manufacturing plants, including a Navistar heavy duty truck assembly plant. *(More on this story in Principle 86).*

Similarly, in 2016, the city declined to provide exhibit space for the Daughters of the Republic of Texas' Alamo Library collection, when they were forced to move because the Texas General Land Office replaced them as custodian of the Alamo. I stepped in and reached an agreement to house the collection in the Bexar County Archives building located across Nueva Street from the courthouse. Today over 38,000 Alamo Library documents and artifacts are available to the public along with all Bexar County historic documents.

Move quickly when power is vacated and take the initiative when it will enhance your community.

19

WHEN FACING A MAJOR LEGISLATIVE BATTLE PROCURE A CARDINAL.

In Texas, legislative committee chairpersons are known as "cardinals" because they are powerful.

When I was a freshman House member, I told Judiciary chairman Dewitt Hale that all his committee members supported a bill of mine that allowed law students access in a courtroom.

He said, "That's good work but there is only one vote that counts and that is mine and I don't support your bill."

I eventually changed his mind, but I never forgot the chair's power.

Before each biannual legislative session both the San Antonio City Council and Bexar County Commissioners Court draw up their legislative agendas and work with our local delegation to pass the necessary bills. It is not a good idea to go over their heads and seek sponsorship from an out-of-town legislator. But there are times.

As mayor in 1993, I could not count on our local legislative delegation to pass controversial legislation that regulated pumping from the Edwards Aquifer, our underground water supply. This was necessary to stave off more severe restrictions that were threatened under the Endangered Species Act. Our delegation ducked the controversial issue. I got angry and called them rubberneck chickens. They got kind of mad at me.

Therefore, I had to find a cardinal from another area of the state who would not be subject to pressure from citizens in and around San Antonio. We found the perfect cardinal in Senate State Affairs Committee chairman Ken Armbrister. My friend, businessman Cliff Morton, who I had appointed chair of the newly formed San Antonio Water System, raised funds and fed Cardinal Armbrister the mother's milk of politics, warming the cockles of his heart.

Armbrister drafted the bill, passed it out of committee and then through the Senate and then chose Representative Robert Puente, the only member of our local delegation who agreed to help, to handle his bill in the House. The bill passed and pumping out of the Edwards Aquifer is now regulated. By the way, Puente is now the CEO of the San Antonio Water System.

As county judge in 2007, I needed legislation to create a public improvement district that had unique powers to help fund public infrastructure for a 1,002-room resort hotel and two PGA golf courses and to enhance the environment over the aquifer. Our local delegation was split on the issue because a strong contingent of local citizens were against it on account of environmental concerns over the hotel and golf courses. I thought otherwise because all around the proposed district, nothing was done to save trees and provide green space. The proposed district would have the authority to enhance the environment by setting aside land and passing regulations to protect the environment.

I decided to team up with Kenny Jastrow, president of Temple-Inland, whose company owned the site. He had statewide connections, a strong lobby team and plenty of money. His team lined up the support of key cardinals in the House and Senate.

We were successful in passing legislation to allow our Commissioners Court to create an enhanced public improvement district, the only county in Texas to have this authority. The legislation gave the Commissioners Court authority to create the district, appoint a board to administer it, allowed the board to set environmental regulations, and to collect hotel-motel taxes in addition to property taxes. The hotel-motel taxes could be used to build the golf courses, the hotel, infrastructure and landscaping. Today the hotel and the two PGA golf courses are operating and thriving. Over 800 acres of land was set aside, trees were protected, and strict development regulations were passed.

Seek the power of a cardinal when major local legislation is needed, and your delegation prefers to duck the issue. So, enlist a strong cardinal to get you over the goal line.

20

ACCUMULATE, DISPENSE, AND USE INFORMATION EFFECTIVELY.

Information is powerful. How to collect information and when to use it will determine how successful you will be.

People will spill the beans to a mayor/county executive because they want to be your confidant, even seek to be indispensable to you. It gives them status if they are well connected to power. So, seek and use any valuable information you may pick up from them.

I have picked up information over the years at community meetings, lunches, groundbreakings, and evening receptions. Evening receptions are the best because people are drinking, and the roosters and hens are singing. I do not drink because I need to be on my toes and alert.

I first encourage people to talk about themselves. Everybody likes to do that, and it makes them feel comfortable. They appreciate it because you care about them and that makes them feel good. As they loosen up, I then probe them for any worthwhile information they may have. I hold the information close to my chest and use it to my advantage at the right time.

Reporters are a particularly great source of information.

Nothing is more tantalizing than gossip, and they have gobs of it.

If I want the information to be public, I simply share it with friends. Secrets have a short life in politics because people cannot resist passing it along because you are the source. Therefore, if it is to your advantage, plant information, fertilize it and let it spread across rows of folks.

For example, during my term as mayor, at one evening event I learned from Jude Valdez, the vice president of downtown development for UTSA, that UT system Chancellor William Cunningham was only giving lip service in support of a UTSA downtown campus. For years we had worked hard to have a downtown campus, giving inner city, less affluent students a more central campus as well revitalizing downtown.

When Cunningham came to visit, I refused to sit at the head table with him at a San Antonio event and I would not take his phone calls. Instead, I spread the word of his duplicity by working the phones, calling Governor Ann Richards, telling local business leaders and legislators of his dubious commitment.

Finally, the pressure worked, and he publicly committed to the downtown campus. The campus was built and today expansion is underway under the leadership of UTSA president Taylor Eighmy.

At another evening reception when I was mayor, an assistant district attorney said that he thought that the chairman of our public transit authority, VIA Metropolitan Transit, would be indicted in a case of sexual harassment. I used this information to call for his resignation. This upset his political supporters. The uproar soon settled down, as he was later indicted and then convicted of "official oppression." My early action put politicians on notice that if I spoke out, I had information to back it up.

During the COVID-19 pandemic in June 2020 I spoke with

Craig Boyan, CEO of HEB supermarkets. He told me that he had talked with Governor Abbott's Chief of Staff Luis Saenz and told him that HEB and other businesses supported a mandate requirement that people wear face masks in their stores. With other pieces of information that I gathered I came to the conclusion that Governor Abbott would not oppose an emergency order if I were to issue one.

I quickly issued an emergency order that required all commercial entities providing direct goods and services to the public to develop and implement a health and safety policy that included, at a minimum, that all employees or visitors must wear face coverings. The policy notice had to be posted in a conspicuous location to provide notice to employees and visitors. A fine, not to exceed $1,000 per violation, would be assessed to those businesses that failed to comply.

Abbott then announced he would not oppose the order. Other large counties then also issued one.

By staying alert, seeking information, and using it to your advantage you will be able to take action at the appropriate time, thereby enhancing your power.

21

WHEN YOU LOSE BIG, PIVOT BIG.

Success is a shadow and is soon forgotten but failure lingers to haunt you. A major defeat undermines your credibility with the public and can lead to a bad run of cards. To regain your balance, you must cover your loss by quickly pivoting to win on another major issue.

The city's proposed Applewhite reservoir, located on the Medina River south of the city, had been defeated by the voters with 51 percent of the vote in May 1991, at the end of Mayor Cockrell's term. This would have been San Antonio's first surface water source, relieving our dependence on the Edwards Aquifer.

As mayor in 1994 I sought to revive the reservoir issue by proposing to add reuse water along with the Medina River water to make it a constant level reservoir. We went to the voters again. During the campaign I heard repeatedly, "What is it about 'No' that you do not understand?" Voters again rejected the building of the reservoir.

After losing that vote in May 1994, I quickly pivoted and led the council in enacting an ordinance to protect the Edwards Aquifer Recharge Zone where our underground aquifer is recharged. The 29-page ordinance preserved natural floodplains, kept sinkholes open, used vegetation to filter urban pollutants, and prohibited filling stations over the recharge zone. This was the first ordinance ever passed to protect the recharge zone.

After the victory, people forgot about my Applewhite loss.

In 2014, Mayor Ivy Taylor withdrew her support of a controversial downtown streetcar project, and I joined her at a press conference to announce the project was dead. *(Story is in Principle 53).* It was a major defeat for me after working five years on the project. I could not find a strong pivot and as a consequence I faced strong opposition in both the Democratic primary and the general election in the same year. Fortunately, I won and then had time to pivot to other major issues.

A crushing loss can define your term of office unless you act quickly to revitalize your leadership by successfully taking action on another major issue that voters approve of.

22

DO NOT GET CAUGHT CRYSTAL GAZING.

I have always had trouble with this "vision thing." Is vision a dream, a trance, a supernatural revelation, a product of your imagination, or crystal gazing? Or all of them? I am not sure, but I know that reality jumps in the way of aspirational dreams.

In 2002, Mayor Ed Garza, like Don Quixote, drew his sword, saddled up his Rocinante and rode south of the city identifying several thousand acres of land for a new urban mixed-use development. He had a vision of houses with front porches, back alleys, small lots, and close to retail and commercial development.

He spent four years working on it, but nothing happened, and for good reason. It was an expensive planned development in a low-income area of the city with few amenities, inadequate utilities, and poor schools. He offered no incentives to developers to overcome the shortcomings of the site. This was a clear case of crystal gazing.

In contrast, in 2009, Mayor Julian Castro developed a "Housing First" strategy to revitalize downtown. It was not crystal gazing because he made it a reality by setting up a $75 million incentive fund. That led to approximately 10,000 new living units within 10 years.

The 1952 city charter set council member compensation at $1040 per year with an additional $3000 for the mayor. This prevented anyone who wasn't independently wealthy or at least married to someone with a good income from running for city office. It was a throwback to days long gone when service on the council was a part-time job.

Mayor Taylor publicly said that the compensation for mayor and council members was too low. Even though voters rejected pay increases in 2004, she raised money for a campaign and on May 9, 2015, she successfully convinced voters to approve increasing the mayor's pay to $61,735 and the councilmembers' pay to $45,722, San Antonio's median household income according to the 2010 census.

Castro and Taylor were not crystal gazing because their ideas were realistic, and they stepped up with funds to implement their proposals. Garza had on rose-colored glasses and was left with an empty pocket.

You need a reality check before you go off spouting your dreams and vision, giving false hope to citizens. If you cannot deal with the real world and make it happen, then keep your dreams to yourself.

23

WHEN FACING A CHOICE BETWEEN TIME AND MONEY, CHOOSE TIME.

In 2006 we received only one bid on a joint county/city project in cooperation with the San Antonio River Authority that would restore a 1.5-mile stretch of the San Antonio River between Brackenridge Park and the northern end of our world famous Riverwalk downtown. It had been an overgrown eyesore when it should have been an amenity catalyzing economic development along a major corridor north of downtown.

When the cost was twice as much as projected, I thought we should re-bid, but Mayor Phil Hardberger, who initiated the venture, thought we should move forward.

At a meeting in my office in March 2006 Hardberger asked me, "How much did the Taj Mahal cost?"

I answered, "I have no idea."

He replied, "Who cares?"

I said, "Let me think about that."

The more I thought it about the more I realized that Hardberger was right. The political will to build a major project is subject to timing and Hardberger would soon leave office due to term limits. It could also lead to losing the right contractor with experience. Local contractor Zachry Corporation was reliable and available and could get the job done on time.

Later I told Hardberger, "Let's get an independent evaluation of the fairness of the cost from a reputable engineering firm."

PBS&J Engineering found the bid was fair and reasonable under the terms that we imposed. So, we moved ahead with the project.

Over the long term, landmark capital projects are judged by their quality, their significance to the community, and the economic development they generate. If a project is worthy, you will get a return on investment. If time is of the essence in completing the project, then cost is the least determining factor.

The northern reach of the river eventually generated tremendous economic development. Had we chosen money instead of time, the project might not have happened.

Time has its constraints, and time can run out. So, choose time over money when facing a choice.

24

WHEN YOU DON'T HAVE THE HORSES,
WAIT THEM OUT.

From the end of World War II through the 1980s, suburban developers had free rein in San Antonio. As a result, over-development on the north side threatened to contaminate our underground aquifer. However, the mayor and City Council were afraid to take on the developers because of their financial and political power.

After winning the mayoral race in 1991, I did not initially have the votes to pass a comprehensive aquifer protection ordinance. Instead, I took incremental steps to protect the environment. First, we passed a new master plan that set a road map for the implementation of urban design, natural resource protection, and growth management. We scored a first down.

We then started passing ordinances one at a time to implement the master plan. We created urban corridors that set standards for green space, limited signs, and set building setbacks. We passed a landscape ordinance and required builders to bury electrical lines in new subdivisions.

As I mentioned in *Principle 21*, near the end of my term, we also passed the first ordinance in San Antonio's history that put new restrictions on development to the north to protect the Edwards Aquifer recharge zone, our major source of water.

Additional incremental steps continued under later-mayors and still there is work to be done on these issues.

As County Judge in 2001, I made a proposal to the Commissioners Court to restore our historic 300,000 sq. ft. courthouse. My wife Tracy agreed to raise private funds to supplement county funds. It took us over 20 years to complete the restoration because of judges who did not want any changes that affected their courtrooms, as well as the Commissioners Court's reluctance to stand up to their pressure.

For example, it took 16 years to finally get Commissioners Court approval to remove two large inappropriate additions to the courthouse, and that was only after two commissioners had been replaced.

By the end of my 22-year term the courthouse has been restored to its original glory. *(More on this in Principle 37).*

As I mentioned in *Principle 19*, we passed legislation in 2017 establishing a unique public improvement district to build a resort and two PGA golf courses. But it was a six-year long struggle to overcome the environmentalists who had collected 77,419 signatures on a petition to stop the building.

When you do not have the horses, act incrementally or wait them out and find the appropriate time to take action. Patience will win the game.

25

A MOTION TO DELAY IS A MOTION TO KILL.

As mentioned in the previous principle, you must wait them out when you do not have the horses. However, if you do have them, motions to delay can still hobble your horses and perhaps kill them. Too often a council or commissioner member will seek to delay saying they have not had time to study the issue, or they do not understand it when in fact they really want to kill it.

Commissioner Tommy Calvert used every tool in his kit to delay county funding for the Alamo Museum to be built in the restored Woolworth building across from the Alamo. *(More on this project in Principles 44 and 70).* He also tried to stop the creek renovation program in 2021. *(Refer to Principle 90).*

I knew he had reservations about telling the full story of the Alamo, but I had no idea why he opposed the creek plan. But I knew if we delayed, opposition could increase, so I pushed forward with a vote. Interestingly when he had to vote, he voted in the positive.

Over a five-year period, with funding in hand, VIA, our metropolitan transit system, continued to delay starting the downtown streetcar project that they had approved. The streetcar would be the first link in creating a citywide rail passenger service. As time passed opposition grew so strong that the project was abandoned. *(Principles 21 and 53).*

In December 2022, new Precinct 3 Commissioner Grant Moody sought to delay the funding for the "Spirit Reach" of the San Antonio River, which would extend the restoration and beautification of the river through Brackenridge Park to its headwaters on the campus of the University of the Incarnate Word. The connection to the "Blue Hole," the headwaters of the San Antonio River, was critical to completing all the work along the river that we had already accomplished.

This was a project that we had worked on for over 10 years and already had signed contracts with the university and the San Antonio River Authority. Knowing the opposition we had previously faced from the nearby River Road neighborhood, who didn't want any more "outsiders" attracted to the area, I pushed forward with a successful vote.

Delay by staff in implementing a Commissioners Court or City Council decision can also kill a project. Cost of the project can increase, or other circumstances can arise to kill the project. I kept a list of my important projects and stayed on top of staff to complete contracts and projects.

Delay can kill your initiatives. So, when you have the horses push ahead and get the deal done.

26

DON'T LET FEAR OF FREE SPEECH AND ASSEMBLY CHANGE WHO WE ARE.

In the spring of 2018, I participated in a meeting with local officials that included Mayor Nirenberg, former mayor Phil Hardberger, and Ron Kaufman, who was heading up the Republican Party search committee to select a city to hold the 2020 Republican National Convention. Kaufman encouraged us to make a bid and said we would be a favorite to win.

Several local officials, including Hardberger, expressed concern about possible riots because of the animosity President Trump stirs up. Kaufman responded by saying that Trump would be in San Antonio for only an hour. He also assured us that over $40 million in federal dollars would be available for security.

Although I am a Democrat and cannot stand Trump, I spoke up and said we should offer to host the convention. I said our city should embrace the first amendment rights of free speech and assembly and that those rights should prevail over any fear we have of Trump. My voice was a minority.

Later, the City Council in a closed-door meeting chose not to make a bid. Mayor Nirenberg announced that it was because of the financial cost to the city. But most people, including me, thought it was really fear of Trump and his supporters.

It turned out that it did not matter because in 2019 COVID-19 emerged and officials prohibited large gatherings such as a political convention. But in 2023, Houston Mayor Sylvester Turner, an African American Democrat, successfully attracted the 2028 Republican National Convention. He realized it would be an economic boom for Houston.

Later, in the summer of 2020, during the height of the COVID-19 pandemic, fear did not stop us when people from other cities joined local citizens in San Antonio to march and protest the killing of George Floyd by police in Minneapolis. Many citizens thought Mayor Nirenberg and I were wrong in standing up for their right of free speech and assembly. They feared riots might occur as well as the danger of COVID-19 spreading because of the crowds.

On May 29, a few of the protesters broke storefront windows on Houston Street. Police officers responded and by 10:30 p.m., the contested section of Houston Street appeared to be cleared of the small group of protesters. The streets were left littered with garbage and shards of glass.

Four days later, on June 2, a few protestors came to a face-off with police officers around 11:00 p.m. near Alamo Plaza. The demonstration escalated and officers used pepper balls, smoke, and wooden and rubber projectiles as protesters ran away.

So, we did have violence, but no one was seriously hurt. In this case, we did not let fear stop us from allowing freedom of speech and assembly in our city.

Two years later, in 2022, Mayor Nirenberg and I both attended a protest rally held at Main Plaza against the decision overturning the Roe vs. Wade by the Supreme Court. We had no problems with violence.

Stand up for citizens' right to freedom of speech and assembly, even if it is not to your liking. This right should not be abrogated to fear.

27

DON'T LET PROCESS EAT YOU UP.

Process is a series of actions or events that hopefully leads to a proposed result. Too many task forces, too long public hearings, endless council and commissioner meetings, needless studies, and too many consultants can grind away at you and get you lost in the process. The minutiae of processes can leave you with nothing but wasted time and little accomplishment.

When I became county judge in 2001, the Commissioners Court meetings would go on all day long once a week. In addition, a capital projects subcommittee of two commissioners held meetings with staff once a week that also went on all day long. The results were that staff lost two days of work while catering to the commissioners. Drawn out process also slowed down commissioners getting any serious work done on major issues.

First, I encouraged commissioners to meet with staff before the court meeting and get their questions answered. I stopped other elected county officials from putting items on the agenda unless two commissioners signed off.

To move public hearings along I instituted a three-minute limit on the citizens to be heard. I also did not let a dialogue begin between the commissioners and the speakers. I emphasized that we were there to hear the input from citizens and not to get into a debate with them.

I then convinced the Commissioners Court to disband the capital improvement subcommittee. Instead, presentations of only new capital projects were made to the full Commissioners Court. Modifications to funding projects were put on the "consent agenda." They would be passed as a group without discussion unless a commissioner flagged them for individual consideration.

Staff was now able to spend more time getting their work done and making professional decisions, rather than political ones urged by commissioners.

I also limited the number of consultants who compile lengthy studies. Instead, I required staff to search for current studies already underway on the subject. *(You can read about my view on consultants in Principle 34).*

I also set up an expedited system to make appointments to fill vacancies. *(More on this in Principle 67).*

As much as I criticize process, it is necessary if applied properly with due consideration and efficiency. Public hearings, gathering and dissemination of information, council/commissioner debate are all necessary but need to be conducted in an effective and efficient manner.

Don't get lost in the weeds. Focus on expedited processes that will lead to meaningful results.

28

EXPECT THE UNEXPECTED.

As mayor/county executive, you live with uncertainty every moment. Natural disasters, virus outbreaks, mass shootings, and terrorist attacks can come your way at any time. When an unexpected moment hits, you must be prepared to quickly organize, communicate, and act.

Over the years, I have responded to numerous disasters - the terrorist attack of September 11, 2001, the AIDS pandemic, a possible Ebola outbreak, mass shootings in nearby communities of Uvalde and Sutherland Springs, and COVID-19.

The COVID pandemic of 2020-2022 was my greatest test of leadership in an unexpected crisis. Although we think of New York and west coast cities as the epicenters of the pandemic, San Antonio was actually the first place to have to deal with it.

Ninety-one American citizens who had been in Wuhan, China, where the COVID outbreak began, landed at Lackland Air Force Base in San Antonio on February 7, 2020. Ten days later 144 passengers from the cruise ship *Diamond Princess* were flown in. They were all quarantined for 14 days, enough time for COVID-19 symptoms, such as coughing, fever and fatigue to emerge.

Mayor Nirenberg and I quickly assembled a team of health experts who made several recommendations to us, one of which was to establish a working team of health experts, which we did.

On February 29, the CDC mistakenly released a patient who had tested positive. Soon afterwards she went shopping at North Star Mall on the north side of the city. The mall closed for 24 hours and sanitized all their shops and fixtures. The incident led to the first emergency order that Nirenberg and I issued which prohibited the release of any of the evacuees into our community.

Once it was clear that we would be facing an outbreak in our community, we set up daily conference calls with public health officials. Hospital CEOs, law enforcement officials, scientists, and others would occasionally join us on the call.

As we conferred, we each had a daily Situation Report before us prepared by staff. It included how many COVID-19 patients were in the hospital, including a breakout for ICU and those on ventilators, and how many additional staffed beds were available. It also included COVID-19 testing results, nursing home outbreaks, and the number of deaths.

From the information we received, we developed a matrix that measured testing, contact tracing capacity, positive infection rate, hospital stress, and the doubling rate of infections. From that data, we developed a risk level chart ranging from critical to severe, steady, moderate, and low risk. The data and analysis drove the 30 emergency orders that Mayor Nirenberg and I issued over the next two years.

Effective and frequent communication with citizens is critical to gaining citizens' support to help control the spread of a virus. On March 27, 2020, Mayor Nirenberg and I started hosting a live broadcast on local TV news at 6:13 p.m. With three cameras facing us, we spoke directly to the people as each camera alternately took close-up shots of us.

After Nirenberg gave highlights from the daily situation report, I would then provide a commentary. We then took questions from members of the media.

Over the course of the pandemic, we held some 400 conference calls with experts, reviewed 616 daily situation reports and held 319 live broadcasts as well as several press conferences.

We also issued 30 emergency orders during the crisis that were written by City Attorney Andy Segovia and Bexar County Chief of the Civil Division in the District Attorney's office, Larry Roberson. They ranged from closing businesses unless they were essential, to limiting public gatherings, requiring face masks, mandatory health safety initiatives for businesses, and curfews. Fines were assessed against violators and were enforced by the police department, sheriff's deputies, health and building inspectors, and the courts.

Dr. Juan Gutierrez, the chair of mathematics at UTSA, ran a model that showed our early response had prevented an explosion in the number of cases. He said they would have been significantly higher if Mayor Nirenberg and I had not acted early.

As of March 2023, the third anniversary of COVID-19, the virus is still spreading with the death toll reaching 7 million people worldwide. But most of us are living a normal life now thanks to vaccines and immunity derived from previous infections. Two months later the World Health Organization declared the pandemic emergency was over but warned that deaths and illnesses from Covid were still occurring from a new mutation, "Kraken," a derivative of the Omicron mutation. And still another derivative, dubbed "Pirola," has been indentified. It has 30 mutations of the spike protein, which helps the virus enter cells and cause an infection.

It is estimated that several million Americans are living with long COVID (over three months). Symptoms such as fatigue, brain fog, and shortness of breath continue to linger.

By the way, I wrote a book, *The Mayor and the Judge*, which recounts the two-year local war against COVID. Go buy it.

When facing an unexpected crisis, quickly assemble experts, develop a plan, organize your response team, communicate with the public and issue emergency orders with teeth. Be ready to lead for an extended period of time.

CREATE AN EFFECTIVE MANAGEMENT STRUCTURE

29

DE-MATRIX.

As I mentioned in *Principle 13*, it took me a while to find and enhance sources of power embedded in our fractured county government. Former County Judge Cyndi Krier warned me when I took office that county government had a good system of checks and balances, but that it was hard to find accountability.

While the City Council had no management authority, the Commissioners Court has authority to manage departments that are not run by separately elected county officials such as the sheriff, district attorney, and judges.

When I became county judge in 2001, I inherited a confusing matrix system with executives' reporting lines crisscrossing each other. Ten department heads reported directly to the five members of the Commissioners Court, creating a chaotic system.

With 10 executives reporting to five commissioners the matrix system was chaotic. I first put together the votes to weed out weak executives and hired top-notch people to take their place. I replaced a worn-out Budget Director, an unqualified Infrastructure Director, an ineffective Director of Social Services, and a slow-moving Director of Information Services. We brought in better qualified department heads by offering better salaries and working conditions. While I wanted to establish a county manager, I could not get the votes of the Commissioners Court. They liked having authority over numerous county executives. They also argued that no county government in Texas had a county manager.

So, in January 2004, I convinced the commissioners to create a new Chief of Staff position for my office. He would have the authority to do staff evaluations and conduct staff meetings, but not have the authority to hire and fire. I chose Seth Mitchell, the county's intergovernmental manager. It was a step in the right direction, but only a step.

Straight lines of authority are necessary to have effective, responsive management. So, de-matrix.

30

APPOINT A THOMAS CROMWELL AS YOUR COUNTY MANAGER.

While a city manager has clear authority over the entire city bureaucracy, a county manager has only limited authority. They have no control over separately elected county officials that have management authority over their employees. So, they must have the skills to find a way to ride herd over the numerous elected county officials, and bifurcated departments that are shared with the state.

I needed a Thomas Cromwell to manage this kind of mess. Thomas Cromwell, the First Earl of Essex, was the chief minister to King Henry VIII. Cromwell became Henry's most powerful minister as he managed the bureaucracy and carried out the policy and decisions of the king no matter how difficult or controversial.

When former Lord Chancellor Thomas Moore opposed the king's decision to separate from the Roman Catholic Church and establish the King as the Supreme Head of the Church of England, Cromwell charged Moore with treason and oversaw his execution.

I finally was able to count on one vote to establish the office of county manager when my son, Kevin Wolff, a Republican, was elected County Commissioner in 2008 and took office in 2009. Kevin had been an executive with Citibank and understood corporate structure and accountability. But we needed a third vote, and it took a while to get it.

One spring evening in 2011, over dinner, he and Commissioner Paul Elizondo agreed to support the appointment of Budget Director David Smith, as a county manager. I was delighted. Smith was used to taking heat as the budget director and did not cave in to requests for additional funding by county elected officials. Paul and I had worked together with Smith for 10 years and had confidence in him. In the early summer of 2011, the Commissioners Court appointed him county manager, the first county manager in the state of Texas.

We gave him the authority to hire and fire, to set pay, reorganize the departments to create straight lines of authority and hold executives accountable for results. With straight lines of authority, we were able to operate efficiently and fast.

Additionally, we also authorized him to continue as budget director and to hire outside experts as well as additional staff to help him review elected officials' staffing, salaries and work product. Dealing with elected officials required negotiating skills and a tough hide.

Smith became the man to say "no" to elected county officials based on his staffing studies, giving the Commissioners Court a buffer and a reason to deny the requests.

Most important, he was loyal to the Commissioners Court and me. When I had major proposals, he supported them and then worked to complete them.

Smith proved to be as effective, tough and loyal as Cromwell was. While Smith was loyal, he has not gone as far as Cromwell. Smith was smart enough to know that five years after Cromwell executed Moore, Henry VIII had Cromwell executed as well.

As of 2023 Smith continues to serve as county manager under the leadership of my successor, County Judge Peter Sakai.

You need a tough, skillful, loyal manager willing to take the heat from the numerous elected county officials. Best to give him budget authority as an additional weapon to cut through the maze of county government.

31

BREAK UP THE CRIMINAL-INDUSTRIAL COMPLEX.

Judges who handle criminal cases are elected and depend on contributions from criminal defense attorneys and bail bondsmen who seek to delay justice because they make more money the longer a decision is pending. As a result, our local judges were taking, on average, three times longer to dispose of criminal cases than the American Bar Association recommends.

Thus, 60 percent of county jail inmates were awaiting trial for as long as a year, costing taxpayers $75.00 a day for each jail inmate. Several studies have shown the longer nonviolent people sit in jail, the more likely they are to be influenced by dangerous criminals. In 2005, to break up what I considered a system that thrived on money from defense lawyers, bail bond profiteers, jail builders, food vendors, and the list goes on, I persuaded the Commissioners Court to create a criminal justice department.

Through the department we implemented a vigorous multi-level program to bring efficiency to the criminal justice system. We provided judges assistance to better manage their courts. But most important, we decided to throw a little light on them by setting up a transparent system to judge the judges.

We measured the efficiency of each judge, ranking each on the number of cases handled and the time taken to conclude the case. Quarterly reports to Commissioners Court on the rankings were made available to the San Antonio Bar Association and the public. This provided voters a report card on how well each judge ran his or her court in comparison to the others.

Over the years, the gap narrowed between the best and worst judges, taking them all to a higher level of effectiveness and efficiency. Judges worked longer hours, enabling them to handle more cases. They also reset fewer cases. The system began to move more efficiently.

I had another problem with judges. The criminal district judges appointed magistrates who refused in almost all cases to use personal recognizance bonds for minor offenses. As much as I complained, I received no response from the judges.

This had tragic consequences. On July 17, 2018, Janice Dotson-Stephens, who had a history of mental illness, was charged with misdemeanor criminal trespass. Not able to pay her cash bond, she spent nearly five months in jail before dying there on December 14, 2018.

On April 18, 2019, Jack Michael Ule, another homeless and mentally ill person, died in jail after being arrested for misdemeanor criminal trespass. He could not afford to pay his bond of $500.

I now had two good reasons to fight the judges who appointed the magistrates. Over their objections I persuaded the Commissioners Court to defund their appointees and contract with the city for magistration services. In the first month the city magistrates released 29 percent more low level offenders on personal recognizance bonds than in the same month the previous year.

Finally, after a year of political pressure from community

activist groups, the criminal district judges signed a resolution supporting magistration reforms. I was happy they finally got the message. We then authorized them to appoint new magistrates, subject to the Commissioners Court's ratification. We approved the magistrates only after they stated they supported personal recognizance bonds for minor offenders. They also allowed the district attorney and the public defender to be present and make recommendations at the bond hearings.

In addition to supporting judicial reform, we created a pretrial diversion program for first time youth offenders. More than 770 youths were placed in the program. We hired two additional forensic technicians to speed up the results of drug tests, providing results within 20 days instead of the previous 60 days.

We also embarked on a plan to heal and treat the sick rather than incarcerate them. We established a mental health diversion program, also managed by the department. We gave the police and deputies an opportunity to take an arrested person to a mental health facility rather than jail.

We opened a comprehensive center near the jail that provides housing assistance, job search resources, treatment, and other services for those who had served their time.

We also created mental health and drug courts, a veteran's court, a DWI court, and a "pearl court" helping women who were caught up in human trafficking. Defendants were put on probation, assigned caseworkers, and subjected to frequent drug testing. By 2023 we had 14 judges administering therapeutic courts. Over the last 20 years, we have had thousands of successful graduates of these treatment programs with a recidivism rate of less than 20 percent.

In 2021, the Commissioners Court established a managed assigned counsel program with the support of the judges. No longer did judges face a conflict by naming private counsel and then authorizing their pay and expenses. This was a huge step forward by removing the authority from judges to appoint lawyers for indigent defendants.

Through all the programs administered by the criminal justice department we have reduced our jail population from approximately 4,500 when I took office in 2001 to approximately 4,000 in 2023. During the same time our population in Bexar County has grown by over 500,000 people.

By reforming the criminal justice system we have established an effective management system and saved county taxpayers millions of dollars every year.

Be willing to stand up to the judiciary and demand accountability. Best to create a specific department to deal with the array of multiple criminal justice issues to break up the criminal-industrial complex.

32

DON'T LET LABOR DISPUTES GET OUT OF CONTROL.

After she retired, City Manager Sheryl Sculley wrote a book, *Greedy Bastards: One City's Texas-Size Struggle to Avoid a Financial Crisis*. In it she cited another book written by Ron DeLord, President of the Combined Law Enforcement Associations of Texas. DeLord wrote that when in a labor dispute, a police union should single out a scapegoat and then loudly and consistently claim they are the enemy.

In 2014 Sculley became the enemy after the city could not reach an agreement with the police and fire unions. The police and fire budgets were growing at a rate that would soon consume more than two-thirds of the city's General Fund budget (the part supported by the property tax and other general revenues). This would crowd out all other city functions and jeopardize a lot of City Council's other budget initiatives.

Under an "evergreen clause" the existing contract terms would be kept in effect for up to 10 years if a new contract was not approved. After negotiations had failed to produce agreement on a new contract during the term of Mayor Julian Castro, the city attorney and Sculley recommended the City Council file a lawsuit contending that the evergreen clause was unconstitutional.

The suit was filed even though city officials had signed the contracts with the evergreen clause in them. This was the beginning of a four-year long, very nasty public battle. The escalating labor union dispute descended into destructive politics.

Councilmember Ivy Taylor was appointed Mayor in 2014 when Mayor Castro resigned to take a presidential appointment. Subsequently she was elected for a full term. She teamed up with Sculley to reach an agreement with the police union.

But the fire union said they would not negotiate a new contract unless the city dropped the lawsuit over the evergreen clause. The city chose not to drop it and the fire union decided to fight.

A year after Ron Nirenberg was elected Mayor, in 2018 the fire union launched an all-out assault on the city government that provides their paychecks. They collected enough signatures to put three propositions on the ballot.

One of these would limit the city manager's term to eight years and cap his or her salary at ten times that of the lowest paid city employee - a level that would be completely noncompetitive with other cities our size in future years. Another would grant the union the exclusive right to declare an impasse in collective bargaining negotiations and impose binding arbitration for a new contract. The third would reduce the threshold for a referendum on an action by City Council to only 20,000 votes, holding council decisions hostage to the wackiest of activist groups.

The fire union also ran paid television ads against the city manager complaining about her high salary and attempts to limit police and fire budgets. Following the advice of CLEAT President Ron DeLord, the union unfairly identified Sculley as the enemy. They launched a nasty, deplorable attack campaign which was very unfair to her personally and to the city as a whole.

The fire union won the first two of their charter amendment initiatives in the November 2018 election. The only proposition defeated was the one which would have made decisions by City Council subject to a referendum.

After the loss, Sculley announced her retirement. She had been an outstanding city manager.

The whole debacle could have been avoided, had one of the three mayors stood up and convinced the City Council to drop the lawsuit before the fire union brought forward their initiatives. A few days after the November election, the city finally dropped the lawsuit over the evergreen clause.

Eric Walsh was appointed the new city manager in February 2019. Walsh is a native San Antonian and a graduate of Trinity University's Urban Studies program who was willing to work for less salary than his predecessor because of his commitment to San Antonio.

Mayors should stand up and settle labor disputes before they become a political firestorm.

33

DEVELOP A TEAM OF HOT AND COLD LAWYERS.

The San Antonio city attorney advises the City Council on legal matters. The county district attorney has a team of civil lawyers that advise the Commissioners Court. In addition to city and county staff lawyers, outside lawyers are retained to help on cases that are more complicated. The overall legal team is made up of what I call hot and cold lawyers.

Hot lawyers are those who are aggressive and willing to take chances looking for a legal way to carry out a proposed policy of the governing body when their legal authority is tenuous. Cold lawyers are more cautious and look for every reason to say "no." They are both very useful, but you need to know when to rely on which one.

In 2017, under pressure from a petition drive, the city attorney gave an opinion that the council had the authority to require private businesses to offer paid sick leave to their employees. He was a hot lawyer who carried out the wishes of the council to avoid the petition drive. He gave this opinion to the council even though a state district court and appellate court had already ruled Austin's similar ordinance was unconstitutional.

The council passed the sick leave ordinance and later District Judge Peter Sakai (my eventual successor as county judge) issued a restraining order against it. Six years later the ordinance is still not in effect. Instead of giving in to the petition pressure, the council should have called on a cold lawyer who would have answered they did not have the authority.

In 2007, as County Judge, I found a hot attorney in private practice to advise us that we could expand the use of hotel-motel taxes to build projects never undertaken by Texas counties before. Jim Plummer, an expert in public finance, advised us it was legal to use the tax to build amateur sports parks, a performing arts center and restore the San Antonio River. We later won support from the voters to fund all three issues.

In 2020, I had the help of a great lawyer in Larry Roberson, head of the civil litigation section of the District Attorney's office. During the COVID 19 pandemic, he wrote 60 emergency orders for me. Even when it was questionable whether I had the authority, he stood up for me. For example, as mentioned in *Principle 20* he wrote an emergency order for me that authorized a $1,000 fine on any business that did not develop a health safety policy and post it for customers to see.

Know when you want a hot lawyer and when you need a cold one. Find the right one for the purpose.

34

ONLY HIRE CONSULTANTS TO FIND A WAY TO YOUR END GAME.

In the 1970s, over the objection of my dad, I hired a consultant to advise our family business on how to better manage our growing building material business. My dad thought it was a waste of time and money. He said that if the consultants were any good, they would be working as a business executive or running their own business.

After concluding their study, May Consulting firm advised my dad that my brothers and I did not have the experience to run a growing company and that we should be replaced by professional managers. Dad looked at me and laughed and said we will do that tomorrow. I felt like a knucklehead. But Dad was only kidding.

Contrary to the consultant's advice, my brothers George and Gary and I were very successful. We built more stores and then in 1977 sold all the stores to a national company for several million dollars.

I learned my lesson and now the only time I hire consultants is for their expertise to get me to my end game. As county judge, we hired a team of engineering consultants to find a way to restore San Pedro Creek. The creek runs through the west side of downtown and for years had been an eyesore confined to a narrow concrete channel. The consultants came up with the right technical solutions and we moved forward. *(Story in Principle 90).*

When we issued bonds, we hired consultants to advise us on the timing, amount, and pricing. We hired technical consultants on numerous issues such as to advise us on the best software to purchase.

But without a clear understanding of what the end game is, consultants can create havoc. In 2017, the City Council hired consultants to develop a housing plan without an end game strategy. The unrealistic billion dollar plan was never implemented. Later in 2022, the council adopted a realistic plan of 14 projects that will build or preserve affordable housing.

Sometimes consultants worm their way into legislation that forces you to hire them. For example, to be able to enact incentives for minority companies under federal law you must prove that your governmental entity has discriminated against them in the past. This required hiring consultants to do a $300,000 study. Both the city and county have commissioned such studies. How stupid is this? But it's a federal law that you must first prove yourself guilty.

By the way, there are a few books that will give you warnings about consultants. One I recommend is Martin Kihn's 2005 book, *House of Lies: How Management Consultants Steal Your Watch and Then Tell You the Time.* Another is Mariana Mazzucato's 2023 book, *The Big Con.*

If you need a consultant to get you to your end game, then hire one; otherwise let them pontificate somewhere else.

35

ADOPT A CONSERVATIVE BUT FLEXIBLE BUDGET.

During my 22 budget years as county judge, we adopted conservative budgets that underestimated revenues, overestimated spending, and carried a large cash balance forward. We created reserves for unforeseen expenses and prioritized capital projects over operations funding. As a result of our conservative policies, we have maintained a triple "A" credit rating from all three credit rating entities.

While our budget process is transparent in terms of the budgeting of funds, it has an inherent complexity with hard-to-understand provisions that are required under state law. Our county manager/budget director David Smith also inserted other provisions that gave Commissioners Court flexibility during the budget year.

For example, we issue certificates of obligation rather than bonds that require voter approval. Therefore, our capital budget items can be reduced, transferred, or delayed. This along with a sufficient contingency fund gave the Commissioners Court power to substitute spending needed for unanticipated items.

Under our adopted county budget, the county manager has the authority to adjust and fund unanticipated personnel changes and expenditures. Any major change is subject to Commissioners

Court approval.

For example, in 2018 the Commissioners Court adopted a $1.7 billion budget. During the year, the court approved budget adjustments totaling $16,428,878. We had a large enough contingency fund and savings from other budget items to fund the adjustments.

Adopt conservative budgets that also give authority to council/commissioners to change certain budget items during the budget year as long as spending is not increased beyond the budget.

36

INSPIRE AND TAKE CARE OF YOUR PEOPLE.

A mayor/county executive cannot be effective unless they have a competent, happy workforce who will promptly carry out their initiatives. Working conditions, pay, and benefits are all important. Just as important is inspiring them to be leaders in taking on major projects passed by the Commissioners Court/City Council.

You have read or will read later all the initiatives that our local council/Commissioners Court have taken that require leadership from the staff. The initiatives create excitement as every employee has a stake in pushing them forward.

Equity is also important, particularly in how you treat your lower skilled employees. Our lowest paid county employees now make $15.00 an hour after we adopted a living wage strategy in 2014. The high minimum wage also has an escalating effect upstream on all other hourly employees. We also measure the pay of employees in a citywide comparability survey every two years.

We raised the county's contribution to our retirement plan by matching the employee's contribution on a 2 to 1 ratio. We have a great health insurance and benefits plan. As a result, employees stick with us.

We have taken major steps to improve the work environment. Over the 21 years and 8 months that I served as county judge we built 10 new buildings, acquired two, and remodeled others, greatly improving our employees' working conditions.

We have less turnover and have established Bexar County as an effective local government that has received numerous awards because of our workforce.

You can proclaim, set policy, and initiate projects, but unless you have an inspired, competent workforce to implement them not much will happen. So, inspire and take care of your people.

37

BUILD A CHAMBER THAT EXEMPLIFIES POLITICAL POWER.

When I became mayor in 1991, the City Council chamber was a crummy small place that held only about 100 citizens. It was dark, crowded, hot and uncomfortable and citizens showed their displeasure by easily losing their temper.

Across the street from City Hall, the city owned a historic 1922, 11-story former bank building that it used for a variety of city offices. It included a three-story high bank lobby with a mezzanine that wrapped around the second story featuring Tiffany lamps on a marble railing. It was a magnificent space.

In 1992, when I proposed to remodel that space as a new council chamber, *Express-News* columnist Roddy Stinson wrote in part, "We are sick of scams and schemes and tired of subterfuge and chicanery. If you have one stamp, write Wolff. He is the chief sly boots behind this Versailles West plan."

Because of the animosity he stirred up, I could not get the votes. I had to wait a year to light up the scoreboard before I was able to get the City Council to agree to fund the plan.

Over the next two years, we restored the original ornamental ceiling that featured floral medallions, repaired damaged cast stone and marble finishes, and rewired and restored the historic Tiffany lights. The marble stairway that had led to the basement was moved and re-installed to reach the mezzanine.

We moved into the new chamber on May 19, 1994. It accommodates up to 454 people and it is one of the most beautiful chambers in the nation.

As county judge, I ran into opposition from local judges when I proposed to restore the original three-story high, 1896 courtroom at the front of the courthouse into the Commissioners Court chamber. The original walls and ceiling had been covered with sheetrock. The balcony had been removed, the porch enclosed, and the floors covered with linoleum. Making matters worse, a floor had been added in the 1960s that divided the original courtroom vertically into two courtrooms.

The judges did not want to move to another location in the courthouse that we proposed. Finally in 2013, I was able to override their objections and we began work on the courtroom. We took out the added floor, restored the original balcony, and opened up the porch facing the front of the courthouse. We restored the original features of the courtroom that included thirteen rose windows and gold fleck molding that had been covered up.

Today the restored 30-foot-high chamber is stunning. We have recreated the grandeur of the courtroom as it looked in 1897. You can feel its power and grandeur the minute you walk in. There is ample room for citizens in a comfortable setting.

We held a grand opening and our first Commissioners Court meeting there on January 6, 2015. The San Antonio Conservation Society presented us an award for the work.

Citizens are proud of the dignity of both chambers and that rubs off on the governing body. Both the council and court chambers are available for community events hosted by various non-profit associations. For example, in 2018, the 300th anniversary of our city, Tracy and I hosted organized a reception for Spanish King Felipe VI, and Queen Letizia in the double height restored Commissioners Court.

Exercising power as mayor/county executive is what the game is about. Power is exemplified in a proper setting and a grand chamber will enhance your authority.

WORK COLLEAGUES WITH HONEY AND SPICE

38

TAKE ADVANTAGE OF NEW COLLEAGUES
FOR THEY KNOW NOT WHAT THEY DO.

When I was elected mayor in 1991, four new councilmembers were also elected at the same time that I was. Because of the newly imposed term limits, four more councilmembers left office over the next two years.

With eight out of 10 councilmembers newly elected or appointed, I had the opportunity to move fast because they did not understand the budget, or grasp the finer points of an ordinance, and did not know the key administrative staff members. They also had not formed opinions on many issues.

I quickly jammed the accelerator on several important proposals. They included a new professional baseball stadium *(Principle 65)*, a new council chamber *(Principle 37)*, doubling the size of the convention center, an Edwards Aquifer protection ordinance *(Principle 21)*, and creation of the San Antonio Water System by combining three different water related agencies.

But when I became county judge in 2001, all four of the commissioners had served several years. There was no jamming the accelerator as I had as mayor because they were already set in their ways and had their own policy positions. I had to work hard for their support, but still managed to accomplish several objectives.

But within four years I had two new commissioners who were more willing to consider new initiatives. I now had the power to move a lot faster and I did. We approved a $500 million 10-year flood control plan funded by certificates of obligation *(Principle 35)*, expanded the role of the department of criminal justice *(Principle 31)*, and began planning for the restoration of the San Antonio River *(Principle 90)*.

Move your agenda fast when you have inexperienced colleagues. When you have more experienced members than you, slow down and work to convince them of the merits of your proposals.

39

ESTABLISH DECORUM, ABSORB THE HITS, AND DEFEND YOUR COLLEAGUES.

In the early 1970s as the youngest member of the Texas Senate, I learned that courtesy to your colleagues is necessary to establish public respect for the governing body. The 31 members of the Texas Senate adhere to custom, protocol and decorum in its ornate chambers where members do not personally attack or denigrate each other.

Even the Texas House, with 150 members, keeps a high degree of decorum. A member who personally attacks another member is put in a sort of penalty box. That means his bills are dead until he apologizes.

As mayor or county executive, you should show respect for your colleagues even when you think they do not deserve it. If one is personally denigrated, eventually your governing body will fall into disrepute.

In a smaller governmental body, such as Commissioners Court (five members) and City Council (11 members), any hint of disrespect by one member to another member is amplified. As presiding officer, I called them aside if they said anything personally about another member. I also called down any citizen speaking before us if they personally attacked a member.

For example, during a court meeting in 2010, I defended Commissioner Sergio Rodriguez when an article in the *San Antonio Express-News* alleged that an email that he sent to his fellow commissioners was a violation of the Open Meetings Act. When I found out that my chief of staff had emailed the *San Antonio Express-News* that the Commissioner did violate the open meetings law, I fired him.

As another example, Councilman Mario Bravo lashed out at councilmember Ana Sandoval on September 15, 2022, after she voted against his proposal on spending CPS Energy surplus funds. Bravo and Sandoval had a previous romantic relationship. He said her actions illustrated why he did not want to have children with her. Mayor Ron Nirenberg took decisive action. The following week on September 22, 2022, Nirenberg removed Bravo from all committee assignments. In November the City Council censured Bravo. In 2023 Bravo lost his re-election to Sukh Kaur, a newcomer to politics whom I supported. She graduated from Rice University with an MBA degree and a doctorate degree from Vanderbilt. She has an education consulting business.

Beyond establishing decorum, it is also important to defend your colleagues by giving them cover on controversial issues. In 2021, I agreed to house 2100 migrant children in the county exposition hall. They had crossed our border with Mexico seeking asylum. When the county came under criticism, I took the heat defending our action. *(More in Principle 78).*

When I issued 30 emergency orders during the COVID-19 crisis, I gave cover to the court by not asking them to support my controversial orders.

While there always will be disagreement on issues, it is important to keep the debate civil. They need to know you will stand up for your beliefs.

Standing up for your court/council will garner you support from your colleagues as well as bringing respect to the governing body.

40

DEVELOP A SYSTEMATIC WEB OF PERSUASION WITH YOUR COLLEAGUES.

In addition to standing up for your court/council members, you must also develop a system of persuasion to move your agenda forward. First, you must know the strengths, weaknesses, and vulnerabilities of your colleagues to understand what will motivate them to support your initiatives.

Spend time with them at lunch, on trips and at evening events, raise campaign funds for them, endorse them, and then campaign for them. Be a playmaker by tossing the ball to your teammates and letting them take their own shot.

For example, I supported Commissioner Rebeca Clay-Flores on her initiative to financially assist water customers who had broken pipes after the hard freeze that Texas suffered in February 2021. In 2020, I supported Commissioner Justin Rodriguez in establishing a $7 million fund for mental health. In 2022, Commissioner Marialyn Barnard took the lead in providing a homestead exemption on county property taxes. I was happy to support them in these initiatives.

I also use the tactics I learned in my first year in the legislature. Early in the session, after voting against a bill that the House leadership supported, my phone started ringing. The message from my best supporters was, "You have to go along to get along. If you want our continued support, get on the team."

Bill Heatley, the powerful chairman of the appropriations committee, let me know if I wanted increased funding for the University of Texas at San Antonio and our U.T. Health Science Center, I had better support the whole budget when it gets to the floor. I suited up for the House leadership team.

Learning from that legislative lesson, I kept a list of my colleagues' financial supporters. I called them for help in pressuring my colleagues for their vote when I had trouble getting it otherwise. Politically active groups such as COPS/Metro, the Texas Organizing Project, and local chambers also helped me in getting votes.

Understand and support your colleagues, but at the same time be prepared to use pressure to secure their vote. Enlist your colleagues' financial contributors and supporters to put pressure on them when you can't get their vote otherwise.

41

DEVELOP AN UNDERBOSS.

A mayor/county executive needs a colleague as an underboss. They have to be like-minded, have total confidence in each other and each have skills to move an agenda forward. Mayor Henry Cisneros (1981-1989) tapped the late Councilman Frank Wing as his underboss. Wing became the arbiter of federal community development funds, the negotiator of the budget, the liaison to staff, and the councilman who put tough votes together. If Wing was headed in a certain direction, you knew he was plowing the field for Cisneros.

As mayor I was unable to develop an underboss because of the extreme two, two-year term limits imposed by voters in May 1991, a month before I was elected mayor. As a result, a constant churning of new council members developed during my two terms as mayor.

But I did develop a strong underboss when I became county judge in 2001. I recognized early on that Commissioner Paul Elizondo was an astute politician when he redistricted State Representative Mike Villarreal's home precinct out of his commissioner's precinct. Villarreal had threatened to run against him. How very clever.

Therefore, I latched onto Paul as my underboss. While I developed, promoted, and implemented major policy initiatives, Elizondo cobbled together financial support for my projects, worked the court and the Hispanic community for support. Paul also helped me in my various campaigns, as I did for him.

We developed a great friendship over 17 years. I miss him terribly after he passed away in December 2018, just a month after we were both re-elected for another term.

A loyal, trustworthy, and experienced underboss will enhance your power like no one else. He or she will allow you to concentrate on creating forward-looking projects and building support within the community.

42

SQUELCH GROUPTHINK BEFORE IT LEADS TO MUSH.

In December 2014, the City Council, pressured by the taxicab industry, debated endlessly in an effort to pass an ordinance that would both keep the cab guys happy and allow newcomers Uber and Lyft to continue to operate. But the ordinance put unreasonable restrictions on the ride sharing companies, causing them both to cancel their ride sharing operations in the city of San Antonio. As county judge I convinced Lyft to keep operating in the unincorporated area of Bexar County as well as the 26 suburban cities.

The city's decision was a blow to the tech industry, sending a message across the country tarnishing San Antonio's image as a tech-friendly city. The decision also deprived citizens of a choice in their mode of transportation.

Finally realizing the harm they caused with their mush ordinance, 14 months later the City Council passed a reasonable ordinance that allowed Lyft and Uber to continue to operate.

In 2017 after a long debate, the City Council passed a labor peace agreement governing operators of franchises in the city-owned airport. The agreement gave unions a huge advantage at the airport that they did not have anywhere else in San Antonio. The ordinance was unfair and likely in violation of the state's "right to work" law. It was such a convoluted mess that a few months later, under the pressure of the business community, the council repealed it.

The sick pay ordinance adopted by the council in 2019 that was overruled by the courts *(Principle 33)*, was also the worst kind of mush thinking. *San Antonio Express-News* columnist Gilbert Garcia said it best, "It is a manipulative exercise that plays with the emotions of grassroots constituents. It gives elected officials cover but delivers nothing."

In all three of the above cases, the Uber-Lyft, labor peace, and sick pay ordinances, the mayors never spoke against them but rather voted for the ordinances. A strong mayor would have put a stop to the mush thinking.

In addition to leading to awful decisions, mush thinking also leads to wasted time. Once, in 2019, I let things get out of hand when I allowed a commissioner to put on a show regarding a lack of affordable housing. Instead of offering a solution he and all his speakers overstated the problem while offering bogus studies that were dated. We wasted two hours waddling in mush that led to nothing. My fault.

It is up to mayors and county executives to turn off the burner and stop the cooking when it leads to shapeless, convoluted debate and crazy decisions.

43

TRADE FIVE NICKELS FOR A QUARTER.

"Nickels" are made up of everyday needs that councilpersons and commissioners must respond to in their districts - district offices, roads, streets and sidewalks, enhanced law enforcement in their districts, and numerous other demands.

It is the mayor/county executive's job to support funding for their colleagues' numerous projects. Moreover, when you do, you put a nickel in your pocket for each one you supported.

Over time, you will accumulate quite a few coins. Then, when you make the "big ask" for a quarter, pull out the nickels to remind them of your support for their projects.

My "big ask" as county judge was for major impact capital projects such as the river and creek restoration, the performing arts center, major expansion of our hospital district and other transforming capital projects.

I also used the five nickel-quarter theory when dealing with the city. I was willing to pay more to the city on smaller contracts such as animal control, the police/fire communication system, and restaurant inspections. I was also willing to give the city low prices on services we provided, such as magistrate services, health care services through our hospital district, and rent on county facilities.

In turn, I was able to obtain city land for some of the 13 sports parks we built, land and a building for the county-funded performing arts center, and city funding for restoring bridges on the San Pedro Creek project.

Keep folks happy by being generous on smaller projects as you build up chips for the big ask.

44

RESCUE BIPARTISANSHIP FROM CLANS AND TRIBES.

There was a time when bipartisanship was fostered, respected, and admired. During that time, I had the pleasure to work with several Republicans.

I had worked with Republican U.S. Senator Kay Bailey Hutchinson to secure federal funding to begin the design phase of the Mission Reach of the San Antonio River. I worked with Republican Congressman Will Hurd in securing funding for the new federal courthouse that now has been built a block away from our county courthouse. I partnered with Governor Rick Perry to provide dual rail service for the proposed Toyota plant that was successful. Texas House Speaker Joe Straus defended us on numerous occasions from bills that infringed on local authority.

Bipartisanship gave way when President Donald Trump was elected in 2016. He knew how to scratch the thin, irritable skin of his followers to generate rage in them. Since then, his election compromise has been much more difficult, as the right wing of the Republican party took over. At the same time Trump was elected president, Texas House Speaker Joe Straus did not seek re-election as the state of Texas turned sharply to the right and the Republican party censured him.

Trump considered civility and bipartisanship as surrendering. He divided the nation as he championed conspiracy theories and gained the support of right wing groups such as the Proud Boys.

At a rally in Waco in March 2023 Trump said, "I am your warrior. I am your justice. If you have been wronged or betrayed... I am your retribution."

They responded with cheers looking to him for justice much like the members of a band of Mafia brothers look to the Godfather.

As Texas turned right, he picked up Republican supporters. Trump's biggest supporter, Texas Republican Lt. Governor Dan Patrick, thrives on controversial social issues.

Texas Governor Abbott has better manners but is not much better than Patrick. Abbott had visited our migrant center located in the Bexar County Expo Hall on April 6, 2021. He lied about the center and tried to shut it down. *(Story is in Principle 78).*

Speaker Joe Straus' successor, House Speaker Dennis Bonnen was recorded as saying in 2019, "Any mayor, county judge that was dumb ass enough to come meet with me, I told them with great clarity, my goal is for this to be the worst session in the history of the legislature for cities and counties." He was speaking of Democrats who represent all the urban counties and cities.

Politically we are becoming much like clans and tribes, loyal to their leaders regardless of their lies, unethical, immoral, and even criminal behavior. These leaders espouse a convoluted ideology that is almost Orwellian. It captures an innocent person's mind with propaganda, disinformation, denial of truth, manipulating the past, and double-think: liberty is censorship, freedom is subjugation, and democracy is despotism.

Perhaps even more dangerously there is a reverse feed from

the crowd to Trump-like office holders. The worshiping crowds assure them that their acts are good in their own eyes as well as others. They become more assured of themselves by inoculating themselves from seeing themselves as evil.

I have found trying to work with hard core right wing Republican legislators is vexing and results in failure most of the time. But in spite of the frustration, I still try to search for that 10 percent we could agree on.

Lt. Governor Patrick abhors the bad manners of a solicitor who has not sent a political contribution. When Commissioner Trish DeBerry and I met him at our migrant center a couple of weeks after Abbott had lied about our center, I had to find another way to display my good manners.

Patrick was a big supporter of the Alamo restoration and so was I. I told him that I would persuade the county to contribute $25 million over five years to match an additional $50 million in state funds. With Commissioner DeBerry's support, the Commissioners Court approved the funding. He appreciated my manners, and by the way, he never criticized our migrant center.

I hope that voters will finally realize that bipartisanship is necessary to strengthen our nation and states. If they don't then Democrat and Republican leaders will have to show courage to reach across the aisle. Or an internal fight within the clan will lead to a cleansing of the hard right of the Republican party and the far left of the Democrat party.

Don't burn bridges that can lead to bipartisanship. Keep crossing that bridge and hopefully you will find a route that will lead to others crossing the aisle.

45

MUFFLE COUNTY-CITY DISPUTES.

The public does not like to see city and county officials fighting each other. They consider it a waste of time and local resources. As county judge I had disagreements with the five mayors who served during my term of office, but we tried to not let them become public.

We met bi-weekly to review each other's agenda and helped each other where we could. Over the years together, we created numerous partnerships on various capital projects. We also avoided duplication of services by contracting with each other.

But there are times when disputes become public. As mentioned in *Principle 12*, we acted fast to build the county's all digital public library. As we expanded our locations over the years, we cut the county contribution to the city library system from $3.8 million to $2.2 million. That did not sit too well with the city.

In a front page newspaper article in 2022, city officials criticized a county proposal to build a water link between the San Antonio River and San Pedro Creek. Instead of responding, I said they had legitimate concerns and that we would do a preliminary engineering study and then consult with them as to whether we should move forward together.

During the COVID-19 pandemic, Mayor Nirenberg and I had differences of opinion from time to time, but we quietly worked it out behind the scenes.

Best to muffle disputes, try to work them out, or go your separate ways.

BUILD COMMUNITY SUPPORT

46

DON'T LET LOOSE A TSUNAMI OF TASK FORCES.

In 2018, Mayor Nirenberg and the City Council created task forces on affordable housing, airport development, public transit, and climate change. They put too many academic smarty-pants and wacky consultants in the same room and as a result they rolled out a rambling, chaotic zigzag menu of unrealistic expectations.

The total cost of the plans exceeded several billion dollars. The affordable housing plan cost $1 billion plus yearly administration, the public transit plan $3 billion, airport expansion $2 billion, and the climate control plan did not list cost but could exceed billions of dollars.

Many of the goals in the plans were aspirational. The climate change plan contained a goal that by 2050, no vehicles would be on city streets unless they used renewable fuels. There was no conceivable strategy that the city could implement to reach that goal.

The plans were blurry, unreasonably costly, and too many were bunched together at once. As a result, the policy wonks, consultants, and task force members almost got the mayor chicken-fried in the May 2019 mayoral election. Councilman Greg Brockhouse attacked Nirenberg for over promising and not delivering. He forced the mayor into a runoff and barely lost in the runoff with Nirenberg winning only 51.11 percent of the vote.

While it is important to harness the power of knowledgeable and capable constituents to serve on task forces, they should be given a clear mission that is financially doable within a set timeframe. And do not let too many of them loose at the same time.

Several years later, realizing what was financially doable, Mayor Nirenberg and the council passed a $150 million bond issue for housing instead of several billion dollars.

In 2023 the City Council funded up to $30 million for architectural and engineering services for a new terminal and related projects at the San Antonio International Airport. They also approved a contract for $62 million which includes building a ground loading facility. It will take substantial federal aviation funds to accomplish what is now a $2.5 billion renovation. *(More on this project in Principle 91).*

Overloading the kitchen table with food leaves a lot of leftovers that spoil. So, don't let task forces and consultants run wild with too many issues at one time, thereby spoiling most of the meal.

47

IDENTIFY AND CATCH THE WAVE OF CHANGING POWER BLOCS.

Power continuously shifts among political blocs such as labor unions, neighborhood associations, developers, and business associations. To stay ahead of the curve, you must identify and catch the wave of the changes and tap into new leadership.

Communities Organized for Public Service (COPS) emerged as an inner city power bloc during the 1970s. Then councilman Henry Cisneros tapped into their power as they advocated for capital improvements in poor neighborhoods. That set the stage for his mayoral race.

In my race for City Council in 1987, I was the first candidate to harness the growing power of northside neighborhood associations. They also became the key to winning my 1991 mayoral race. Today neighborhood power is on par with developers, creating a balance of forces.

Around 2010, a new cadre of developers emerged and eclipsed the older edge-of-city developers. They were younger and willing to take the risk to invest in the inner city. The city and county recognized their strength and teamed up with them through public-private partnerships to transform the inner city with some 10,000 new housing units since 2013. Several more are under construction today. The once powerful suburban developers began to lose their influence.

In 2013, a new set of tech entrepreneurs emerged and organized under the banner of "Tech Bloc" to lobby for policies friendly to a tech workforce. Their first issue was to convince the City Council to correct the ordinance that caused Uber and Lyft to leave the city *(as mentioned in Principle 42)*. They were successful. They then encouraged the city and county to create a downtown tech district and offer incentives to new tech companies.

I jumped on their train early by providing county incentive funds for small tech firms and giving financial support to a downtown tech district.

Power also shifted from the Greater San Antonio Chamber of Commerce, which is supported primarily by large companies, to the North San Antonio Chamber and the Hispanic Chamber that are supported mostly by smaller businesses.

The Texas Organizing Project emerged as a political force in 2017 when they gathered 144,000 signatures to demand a popular vote to require sick pay for employees of private companies *(Principle 33)*. I linked up with them in my battle with the bail bond industry *(Principle 31)*. We were successful in getting more personal recognizance bonds approved by the magistrate judges.

Stay alert, get ahead of the changing power structure, and lock into the new.

48

STREET SMARTS ARE IN THE STREETS YOU KNOW.

At a southside event during my 1991 mayoral campaign, Congressman Ciro Rodriquez told the crowd that I knew where the dead-end streets were. The statement had a double meaning. I knew the geography of the neighborhoods but also the dynamics of neighborhood leaders. I understood the complexity of the turf wars between southside politicians and the diverse needs of the neighborhoods.

I grew up on the south side during the 40s and 50s, a time when we kids roamed the streets and became street smart. We developed a self-assured sort of cocky walk indicating we were not to be fooled with. We got to know who the good and bad guys were in a neighborhood.

We learned where the tough neighborhoods were. When passing through one we kept our eyes and ears focused, glancing over our shoulder from time to time. We were friendly but didn't show weakness and most importantly, we did not get caught by any bad guys on a dead-end street.

What I learned on the streets of my youth helped me stay off the dead-end streets of life and gave me the strength and knowledge to handle my opponents. It also reminded me that I still needed to be on the streets of our city.

During my 1987 council race I made sure that I would not be like a stray dog losing his way in neighborhoods he had not visited. So, I walked every neighborhood in my district, talking to people and keeping notes on their concerns. Once I took office, I had a strong team of neighborhood leaders that staffed my council district office as volunteers and followed up on neighborhood concerns.

As mayor and county judge, I continued to walk neighborhoods and attended neighborhood meetings. But obviously, the city and county are too big to reach all of them, so every time I went to an event, I drove through neighborhood streets instead of taking the major arteries. I made notes of code violations as well as street, sidewalk, and drainage problems. My staff would let them know I had been in their neighborhood and that they would follow up on the problems I had observed.

Understanding the texture of the neighborhood and the residents you meet will give you the street smarts to make good decisions on behalf of your citizens.

49

DON'T PUNT TOUGH DECISIONS TO VOTERS.

We live in a republic where elected bodies are expected to make tough decisions on behalf of their citizens. Many times, rather than facing up to a difficult decision, office holders would rather let voters decide. When they do, only a small fraction of voters will likely turn out for the election and hijack decision making.

In San Antonio, some 85 percent of registered voters do not even bother to vote in mayor/council elections. In San Antonio, in the last eight mayor/council elections an average of less than 12 percent of registered voters even bothered to vote. Many times, bonds and referendums are voted on at the same time, but unfortunately there is no increased turnout when they are included on the ballot.

The voter turnout is even lower in special elections. In 2012, 6.7 percent turned out for a city bond election.

Unfortunately, that small cadre of voters can make a bad decision, which could cause a loss in the community's momentum. Over the years public votes in San Antonio have put unreasonable term limits on council members and the mayor, twice turned down the Applewhite reservoir, rejected light rail, and put unreasonable pay restrictions and term limits on the city manager.

Knowing the history of public votes, in 2008 I decided to not call an election to approve a tax increase and issue bond debt to build a new $900 million, ten-story, one million sq. ft. county teaching hospital and a new six-story clinical and ambulatory center. I convinced the Commissioners Court to raise the county hospital district's taxes and issue certificates of obligation instead. *(More on this in Principle 91).*

If citizens did not agree with the decision, they could have collected the signatures of five percent of registered voters and forced a referendum to overturn it, but they did not.

After the Commissioners Court's vote, a constituent called and said that I had a habit of making a decision without getting voters' consent and then later trying to convince people I made the right decision. She was close to right.

You are elected to make hard decisions. Rather than turning to a small cadre of voters to decide the future of the city, make the decision yourself along with your elected body, unless you are mandated to go to a vote by a city charter or state law.

50

PUT THE KIBOSH ON RAISING TAX RATES.

Over the almost 22 years I served as county judge we relied on growing our tax revenue by generating economic development that brought on taxable commercial properties. Because we fostered economic growth and job creation, we were able to reduce the county tax rate from $0.357 per $100 in 2000, the year before I took office, to $0.299 as of 2022, which was a 12 percent reduction. We also passed a homestead exemption and a senior citizen tax freeze. These actions have saved taxpayers approximately $100 million each year.

Taxpayers must curtail spending and live within their means when things get tough. So must local government. Even in times of recession, we held the line on taxes.

For example, in 2007 the Commissioners Court began preparing for what we believed would be a national financial collapse because of the growing fraudulent and misleading packaging of questionable housing mortgages. Realizing we were headed for a blowout, we froze employee positions and curtailed spending on operations. When the November 2008 financial meltdown hit, we were in great financial shape.

At the same time, we continued building the capital projects we had approved when the economy was humming because we had set aside revenue for debt service. These capital projects provided employment to thousands of workers.

Four years later in 2012, the economy began to grow once again, allowing us to add employees and give them raises. Over the four recession years, 2008 to 2012, we never raised taxes.

Managing expenses and controlling the tax rate over the long term fosters economic development, provides governmental stability, and inspires confidence in the citizens.

Keeping the tax rate low and living on the economic growth of the community will inspire more private sector investments and endear you to voters.

51

FOLLOW QUINTUS TULLIUS CICERO'S "RULE OF YES."

Quintus Tullius Cicero was the campaign manager for his brother Marcus Cicero's consul race in 64 BC. In a short paper, he wrote that Cicero would have many people asking him for help and that he should always say "yes," unless a clear obligation prevented him.

Quintus believed that if a candidate made only promises he knew he could fulfill he would not make many friends. If Marcus refused to help, Quintus said the result would be immediate anger. He advised his brother to promise, even though he may be unable to fulfill all the promises. He wrote that some people forget the promise, others may not need the promise to be fulfilled, or the promise could be lost in a cloud of changing circumstances.

Office holders, as well as candidates, should continue to follow Quintus' 2,100-year-old "rule of yes." "No" still incites anger and resentment. The parties you turn down will widely broadcast your lack of care about their cause. Saying no too many times can eventually create a poisoned political climate where you will never be able to govern effectively.

It is best to not snuff out the hope people are looking for. If

I had reason to believe I could get the votes, I said yes. If I was not sure I asked them to help me get the votes.

Interestingly, I found that in most cases my promises did not need to be fulfilled. The political world changes fast and the promised action was no longer needed.

For example, I made promises to match funding for some nonprofit organizations. Many were unable to raise the match. In 2017, I promised Councilman Rey Saldaña to support him if he ran for mayor. He did not run. In 2019, I promised Suzanne Scott, the General Manager of the San Antonio River Authority, to support SARA if the board decided to call an election to raise taxes. They chose not to go forward.

But I turned down financial assistance for a building for a private charter school. It was to my advantage because they were in competition with public education. It would have angered my strong political supporters of public education.

Don't dash hope unless it is to your advantage to do so. Follow the 2,100-year-old "rule of yes."

52

TAKE PEOPLE TO PLACES THEY RESIST OR NEVER ENVISIONED.

In 1963, President Lyndon Johnson's advisors warned him not to move forward with civil rights legislation even though they agreed that the legislation was needed to protect minorities. They told him that Congress and the voters did not want to go there. They asked, "Why fight a losing battle?"

Johnson responded, "Well, what the hell's the presidency for?"

Johnson knew it was the right thing to do and went on to win a historic legislative victory. The same can be said of mayor/county executives: Why take office if you are not willing to take people to a place they resist and may never have envisioned?

When I was a City Councilman, over strong opposition, I supported annexing 23,000 residents into my council district. After they received better water rates, a reduction in the cost of home insurance policies, and better police protection they became happy citizens of San Antonio and the city benefited from the growing tax base.

As mayor over the strong opposition of business leaders I

supported the creation and funding of "Project Quest," an expensive job training program advocated by the inner-city organization Communities Organized for Public Service. Many years later business leaders finally understood quality job training pays off.

In September 2013, Mayor Julian Castro took a bold civil rights step over tremendous opposition when he passed a non-discrimination ordinance to protect the LGBT community. Recall attempts failed. Today the ordinance is well accepted by the vast majority of our citizens.

As I mentioned in *Principle 12*, I led the county effort to build BibiloTech. No one else envisioned what one would look like or how it would function. Today it is an overwhelming success with more than a million people visiting our four digital libraries. *(More about BiblioTech in Principle 87).*

Citizens initially may not want to go where you are taking them or have never thought about it, but when you finish the project and it is to their liking, they will smile and praise it and never admit they were against it.

A trip to the unknown may trouble constituents, so it is up to you to lead them to the promised land.

53

PERSISTENCE IS A CLOSE COUSIN TO STUBBORNNESS.

To accomplish long term, complex capital projects takes consistency and persistence to maneuver through an array of obstacles. When my heart is in a project, I work to overcome all obstacles no matter how difficult and how long it takes. I believe that you can overcome anything by persistence.

You must remain optimistic and fine tune strategies as time passes. I kept pushing, standing up to public opposition along the way as I strove for victory.

Persistence worked for me most of the time. Courthouse restoration took 20 years, criminal justice reform took 22 years, creating a county public improvement district to build the Marriott Resort Center and two PGA golf courses took six years, and redeveloping San Pedro Creek took nine years.

But there are also times when I let my stubbornness blind me to the fact that an issue had been dead for some time. That was the case in my two decade-long effort to create passenger rail service for San Antonio.

As mayor in the 1990s I supported a 16-mile commuter rail line from downtown to the Rim shopping center on the north side. It failed.

In 2000, while I was in the private sector, I was a tri-chair of a metropolitan light rail campaign. We lost that election 2 to 1.

In 2001, as county judge I led the effort to create a commuter rail line between San Antonio and Austin. We entered into a partnership with the Travis County Commissioners Court to create a regional rail authority. After 15 years of frustrating work, we were forced to dissolve the rail authority in 2016 when Union Pacific Railroad withdrew their support.

In 2009, I took the lead in getting the county, the city, and VIA to build a downtown streetcar system as a precursor to light rail. We got off to a good start with over $300 million committed to the project. But opposition built up as VIA dragged their feet in implementing the plan. Five years later in 2014, Mayor Taylor withdrew her support of the streetcar project, and I was reluctantly forced to join her at a press conference to announce the project was dead.

I spent a huge amount of political capital over 23 years on passenger rail projects. As a reward in 2014, I drew two strong opponents, one in the primary and one in the fall, who were both opposed to the rail projects. I won re-election but I paid a stiff price in time, money, and anguish during the campaign.

I worked several years to reform county government by establishing "County Home Rule," the constitutional authority to write a county charter. Then as county judge, I supported merging the city and county in a metro government. Both of those efforts failed miserably.

A stubborn streak does not realize that persistence has its limits. As you keep pushing ahead you may find out you have been among the walking dead for a long time and never noticed it.

54

TAP THE POWER OF RELIGIOUS LEADERS.

My friend Father David Garcia, who is a great priest and community leader, calls me his favorite heathen, because I believe I will return to nature from which I came.

Even though I do not belong to any religious organization, I respect and admire religious leaders like Father David and have worked with them to strengthen our community. Early in my term as mayor, I teamed up with the San Antonio Community of Churches, led by Reverends Kenneth R. Thompson and Ann Helmke, to help our city cope with youth violence. We reached out to youth gangs, condemned easy access to guns, and criticized the entertainment industry for glorifying scenes of violence and drug use.

I partnered with Communities Organized for Public Service (associated with the Catholic Church) and Metropolitan Congregational Alliance, (a progressive organization of Protestant churches) through my mayoral and county judge terms. I joined them in creating the Education Partnership that offered a college scholarship to students who had 95 percent attendance and a B average. I mentioned earlier I supported Project Quest. I also supported their proposed bond issues and their program to grant a $15 per hour minimum wage to all county workers.

When a rock was thrown through a Muslim-owned café after the 9/11 terrorist attack, I joined Christians, Jews and Muslims on the city hall steps to condemn that action.

In 2016, I worked with Doug Beach and Reverend Carol Morehead to host a Pathways to Hope two-day mental health conference. Over 1,500 clergy and parishioners met to help churches create ministries for people with mental health challenges. We have continued the annual meetings. Thousands of people seeking mental assistance have been helped over the last seven years.

In 2016, we opened the county's Reentry Center located near the jail. We provided space and staff support for numerous religious organizations that help former inmates transition back to life on the outside. Chrysalis, Catholic Charities, and St. Vincent de Paul helped with job leads, clothing and transportation.

Tap into the power of religious leaders who are willing to step up to strengthen the social fabric of your city and county.

55

SUPPORT THE SMALL WHO THINK BIG.

The 26 suburban cities in Bexar County are small, encompassing a total population of about 300,000 citizens. As county judge, I had quarterly meetings with the suburban mayors and their city managers. This forum has evolved into a political network that enhances the power of individual mayors.

Some of the mayors are creative and have made a big impact on their cities' economic development. In 2005 Jack Leonhardt, the mayor of Windcrest (population 5,600), created a municipal corporation to buy the 1.2 million square foot abandoned Windsor Park Mall located on 69 acres of land. He then leased the mall to Rackspace, a local IT hosting specialist that was founded only six years earlier in 1999.

As county judge, I worked with Leonhardt to put together a package of incentives to support Rackspace. In 2008, they moved into the building. Some 3,000 people worked for Rackspace at the site for 15 years. But over the recent years they have downsized and in 2023 they announced they were moving to a smaller location. *(More about this in Principle 89).*

In 2012, the county supported the city of Von Ormy in developing a freeport business park on the outskirts of their city. Over

800 people now work in the business park for companies such as Schlumberger, a huge oilfield service company, and a Marachan ramen noodle package factory.

In 2016, the county supported the city of Elmendorf's successful efforts to attract Halliburton's Alamo Junction Rail Park that created 200 jobs. The following year we partnered with them to create tax incentives for a major affordable housing development in the southern part of Bexar County where development lagged.

Working with suburban mayors, we also created an effective voice in the Texas Legislature as we tried to ward off unreasonable restrictions on local government.

Support leaders of small suburban cities when they step up to create economic projects that create jobs and benefit the whole county.

56

FORM REGIONAL ALLIANCES.

What happens in nearby counties impacts your community's progress, whether it is in economic development, road infrastructure, international trade agreements, or climate initiatives.

In the 1980s Mayor Henry Cisneros teamed up with the mayor of Austin to create the Greater Austin – San Antonio Corridor Council, a link between the two cities along 85 miles of I.H. 35. Improvements to I.H. 35 and economic development projects resulted because of the collaboration. Today the San Antonio-Austin corridor is one of the fastest growing economic regions in the country.

In the 1990s as mayor, I teamed up with South Texas mayors and business leaders to form the Association of South Texas Communities, "ASTC." We worked together to successfully fight for the passage of the North American Free Trade Agreement between Mexico, the United States and Canada. We lobbied for increased funding for infrastructure projects that facilitated truck and rail traffic between South Texas and Mexico, our largest trading partner.

As a county judge, I worked with the Alamo Area Council of Governments, our 13-county regional planning organization, to develop a clean air compact to keep the Bexar County region out of non-compliance with the Clean Air Act. We could not have attracted Toyota in 2002 and Navistar in 2020 if we had been thrown into non-compliance.

In the last few years, the private nonprofit San Antonio Economic Development Foundation (rebranded as Greater SATX) adopted a regional economic development policy. The city of San Antonio and Bexar County, that are both members of the organization, supported that effort. For example, they supported adjacent Guadalupe County when they successfully attracted a Caterpillar manufacturing plan and Aisin, a Japanese company that manufactures transmissions.

In May 2023 my successor, County Judge Peter Sakai, announced that Bexar County should expand our reach on economic development projects to Laredo, the Rio Grande Valley and Corpus Christi. He said he looked forward to working with other county judges.

The strong regional economy strengthened our city and county. So, team up with nearby counties and cities to promote growth on a regional basis.

OVERPOWER FRIENDS, ENEMIES, HUSTLERS AND OPPONENTS

57

DON'T RIDE WITH OUTLAWS.

"If you ride with outlaws you die with outlaws" is a quote by Captain McCrae in Larry McMurtry's book, *Lonesome Dove*. You are who you run with.

Metaphorically, a politician who likes nice things and thinks that God made money intended for him is tempted to cross the line, and ride and perhaps die with outlaws.

The "Sharpstown Bank Scandal" unfolded during my first year (1971) in the Texas House. It was alleged that legislators had taken stock in the bank and then supported legislation that would in effect remove regulations from the bank.

Four months after the 1971 legislative session ended, Speaker Gus Mutschler was indicted for his role in the affair. Although Governor Preston Smith and Lt. Governor Ben Barnes were never implicated in the scandal, the voters found them guilty by association and they lost their elections too.

Legislators who did not separate from the Speaker also paid the price. Fifty percent of the House members were newly elected in 1972. I had separated from the House leadership before the session was over and criticized them for giving Sharpstown Bank special treatment. I won a Senate race in the same year.

But times have changed. President Donald Trump retains a high rating with Republicans even though on August 1, 2023, he was indicted for attempting to subvert the will of American voters after he lost the 2020 presidential election. The 45-page indictment makes it clear that it's not a crime to lie, but it is a crime to take actions. His actions include organizing fake electors, telling the Georgia secretary of state to find him 11,780 votes to flip the results, trying to get Vice President Pence to block the certification of the election, and inciting the Capitol riot. He may join 541 other insurrectionists who have pleaded guilty or the 58 who have received prison time.

If your political group is threatened by outside forces, you blindly rise to their defense regardless of the truth. The need for collective belonging overshadows truth, and hence Trump is the leading candidate for the Republican nomination.

It is interesting to note that we were warned by James Madison and Alexander Hamilton that demagogues could incite mobs and factions to defy the rule of law, overturn free and fair elections and undermine America democracy.

In 2023, Republicans, who control the House, have refused to remove Congressman George Santos or even reprimand him after he was charged with embezzlement, fraudulently obtaining employment benefits, and filing false federal disclosure funds.

Republican Texas Attorney General Ken Paxton won re-election the previous November, even though he was indicted by a grand jury in 2015 for felony securities fraud, is under investigation by the U.S. Justice Department for another case of public corruption, and was accused of fraud by eight former employers.

Most of those who rode with Santos, Trump, and Paxton won their re-elections as the outlaws prevailed. But there are signs things may change.

Paxton overplayed his hand when the Texas House refused to appropriate $3.3 million to cover a settlement he had reached with former employers over a whistleblower suit. Paxton attacked the Republican Speaker and House members. He said the Speaker was drunk when he presided over the House. He picked the wrong fight.

The House approved articles of impeachment on May 27, 2023 on charges of bribery, abuse of office and obstruction. The vote was 121 to 23 with 60 Republicans joining 61 Democrats. Under state law Paxton was suspended from office pending a Senate trial. Trump and Texas U.S. Senator Ted Cruz defended Paxton and criticized the vote.

Despite strong evidence of criminal behavior, on September 16 the Texas Senate acquitted Paxton on all impeachment charges. Only two Republicans joined the 12 Democrats to find Paxton guilty, resulting in a 16 to 14 vote for acquittal.

Regardless of changing moral values, cling to decency and do not ride with outlaws.

58

USE HUMOR TO DISARM AND DEFLATE YOUR CRITICS.

In the early part of 2012, I reached a verbal agreement with the Federal Reserve Bank of Dallas to buy their building in San Antonio at fair market value. It is located across the street from the Bexar County courthouse. Later they revoked their promise and asked developers to submit bids to build them a new building and agreed to sell them the existing one.

I wrote Richard Fisher, CEO of the Federal Reserve Bank of Dallas, that we would condemn their building if they refused to sell it to us as they had agreed. When the letter became public, he called me and said I was a dishonorable person and that he held me personally responsible for releasing the letter.

I told him I never accept personal responsibility (not true) and that we were moving forward with condemnation. That really got him mad, and he hung up on me.

I then quickly wrote Fisher a letter telling him how much I enjoyed our conversation and looked forward to his next trip to San Antonio. By the way, they finally sold the building to us. It is now the Bexar County Archives Building.

One day in 2007, after a contentious debate on toll roads, an anti-toll road, big, tall cowboy guy angrily confronted me in the courthouse parking yard. I told him to get away from me and he said, "Give me your best shot."

I looked up to a guy twice my size and half my age, and I did give him my best shot: I laughed at him and told a deputy across the street to haul his ass off.

Over the years, I have received several angry calls at my office. One asked my assistant, who appointed me king?

I said, "Tell him it is a hereditary thing."

Another said I was a moron and now I was a loser as well.

I said, "Tell him I resent being called a loser."

Some people love to get under your skin. The opinionated don't know what they don't know and really don't care to know. They simply want to draw you into a heated argument. If you get angry and argue with them, they drag you down to their level and they win. Remember that they are only dust on your shoulder, and you should just brush them off.

I have made that mistake a few times and it did not turn out so good. For example, on June 24, 2020, I was standing in line at a Lowe's Home Improvement store to check out when I saw a big guy arguing with a cashier about my emergency order requiring face masks in stores. He was about 6'2" tall, in his forties, and wearing a t-shirt with an American flag, an assault weapon, and "Combat Iron" stenciled on the front. When I went to him to explain the order, he hit my wrist and then cussed me out. I gave him a piece of my mind, followed him to his pick-up and got his license number. He was arrested the following day. How stupid I was, letting my anger get the best of me.

After I cooled down the next day, I told District Attorney

Joe Gonzalez that I would not support prosecution. I realized that I was going to make him a hero to Trump and his supporters and that would stir up a storm. Gonzalez dropped the case.

Do not grapple, scuffle, or scrimmage with people whose normal temper is one of rage. Keep cool and deflect the attack with humor.

59

RETALIATION IS BEST SERVED ON A PLATE OF OBSCURITY.

People at the right time and place are capable of anything, no matter how deplorable and dreadful the act may be. While humor is a great way to disarm most critics, these kind of folks need to be dealt with in another manner.

As I mentioned earlier, I grew up on the tough, south side of town. We had a desire for payback that is almost as strong an instinct as hunger and thirst. It is said that southsiders who have Alzheimer's forget everything except grudges.

But over time I learned to control my hunger for payback with occasional mistakes. I realized that personal retaliation is a waste of energy and time. It may cut short the sting, but it only scalds your opponent and does not do him in and in some cases backfires on you.

Rather than personally striking back, I simply inscribed them on a list of past due invoices, waiting for the right time for a mysterious pay back through a proxy. When the time comes, they would not know what caused their excruciating pain.

I had the help of my political consultant Christian Archer

who understood the art of political war. He gathered political intelligence, did opposition research, and reached out to others to deep-six my most nasty opponents.

When Republican Judge Tom Rickoff ran against me in 2018, I did not use negative research that we had compiled on him, even though he lied about my record *(story in Principle 77)*. Two years later when he ran for Commissioner Precinct 3, Archer provided the research on him to his opponent. When his unethical behavior as a judge was revealed, he did not know what hit him. He suffered a lot of pain after his second defeat that sent him home for good.

Bob Davis was president of Alamo National Bank when I was a director of the bank in the 1980s. He was arrogant and a disaster, causing valuable employees to leave the bank.

Many years later he was appointed CEO of USAA, a Fortune Five Hundred company, based in San Antonio. Just like at Alamo National Bank, he laid off hundreds of USAA employees. He really got under my skin when he worked to undermine the county's 2008 proposed bond issue by sending his emissaries to bond task force meetings to work against the proposal.

That same year, 2008, some of the former USAA employees told me about unethical information they had gathered on him. Based on Archer's advice I suggested that they present their findings to the Board of Directors. Later they told me they delivered a letter to the board demanding an investigation of the charges and if they chose not to investigate, they would make it public. Suddenly Davis resigned. When it was announced at an employee meeting that Davis was gone, they responded with sustained applause and so did I.

Personal retaliation can backfire. In 1996, Mayor Bill Thornton found out that Councilman Howard Peak wanted his job. He insulted Peak and said he didn't have the guts to run against him. The attack backfired and strengthened Peak's backbone. He ran against Thornton and defeated him in the 1997 election *(More on this in Principle 66)*. Thornton should have developed a cat's paw approach, using political retribution through proxy rather than a personal attack.

Get a trusted political consultant who will devise a plan of payback, through a cloud of obscurity, leaving no fingerprints.

60

CONQUER, EMBRACE, AND ASSIMILATE USEFUL OPPONENTS.

Most of the time a political crime is not of such an egregious nature that is worth the effort to strike back. It is normal that political opponents will run against you, criticize you and oppose your policy initiatives.

They may come at you like waves on a beach but recede like the outgoing tide when you prevail. After defeating them, the tide will eventually wash them back upon the beach again where they will bathe in the sun nursing their wounds and doubting the wisdom of taking you on again.

Like a good parasite, who leaves his host alive, now is the time for you to rehabilitate an opponent, provided you can make good use of him. It also makes sense to embrace some of your enemies because otherwise they will accumulate. You do not want your support to narrow down to blood relatives and paid staff as some Congressmen have experienced.

When I was mayor in 1993, I appointed Cliff Morton chairman of the newly created San Antonio Water System. He had opposed me in both my council and mayoral races. But he was a talented community leader, did a great job as chairman and eventually became a close friend.

Magnanimity in a political race you have won also goes a long way to make use of a defeated opponent. When Commissioner Tommy Adkisson challenged me in the Democratic primary in 2014 and lost, I held a fundraiser for him later to pay off his campaign debts.

He still had ten months to serve on his current term. Much to the amazement of my colleagues, I assimilated him back onto our team for the remainder of his term and he became supportive on key issues.

As new issues and projects emerge, new battles will break out and bring on a fresh batch of piranhas. The cycle goes on and on, so conquer, embrace, and assimilate your opponents when it is to your benefit.

61

GET ANOTHER JOB IF YOU CAN'T WORK WITH PEOPLE YOU LOATHE.

As mentioned in the previous two principles, there are two classes of political opponents that you should treat differently according to the magnitude of their malfeasance. But there is one more category of people who are not your political enemies or opponents, but you would still like to bust their noses.

I loathe members of our congressional and legislative delegations who do not respond to local officials' requests for support of city and county projects. I also can't stand CEOs of large corporations who do not participate in the life and development of our community and in some cases harm our city.

But you must tolerate them for good reasons. A corporation still provides jobs. Members of Congress and the legislature aren't going anywhere and may be helpful down the line. So, bite your tongue.

I bit my tongue when AT&T CEO Randal Stephenson took money from Dallas to relocate their world headquarters from San Antonio to Dallas. Before he left, he had extracted $6 million from San Antonio to support airline flights that he demanded. Every time we turned around there was a new demand from him, and like cows, we marched along to the eventual killing pen.

Although I wanted to lash out, I had to keep quiet because there would be hundreds of remaining employees in San Antonio. We also had several other AT&T executives who retired and stayed in San Antonio, some of whom have remained active in the community, donating and serving on nonprofit boards. Others went to work for local companies.

So, as county judge, I kept my feelings to myself, hoping the day would come when AT&T would can Stephenson. And in 2019, after several years of falling stock prices and failed acquisitions, it was announced that Stephenson would be leaving AT&T. I danced in the streets.

Working with unresponsive congressional representatives and legislators can also be taxing. Every time I met with Congressman Henry Bonilla, he sat looking at me with a stone face. I was never able to get a commitment out of him for any community project. One day when I saw him outside in the sunlight, I had trouble trying to find his shadow.

State Representative David Leibowitz (2005-11) always thought he was the smartest guy in the room. His condescending attitude turned off people in a meeting. But I had to keep my mouth shut, knowing that his votes could be important to Bexar County.

You must deal with folks you loathe when they hold positions that can benefit your community. Hold your tongue and your nose.

62

WHEN YOU CLEAN HOUSE, EXPECT DUST TO FALL BACK ON THE FLOOR.

After appointed members of boards and commissions have served a while, they tend to create their own separate power structure defying their appointing body. They get carried away with their power and end up making bad policy.

In 2012 members of the Alamo Regional Mobility Authority, an agency charged to finance local highway improvements, refused requests by the Commissioners Court to rein in their prolific spending on administration. We first made a couple of board changes and they promised to change.

Soon after that cleaning, dust fell back on the floor when administration expenses continued to go up to $1 million a year. We used a larger broom this time. We removed all the board members and appointed new members who then released the executive director and staff. The Bexar County Public Works director took over administration at no additional cost and saved over $1 million a year in administration expenses.

In 2016, I began the process of removing members of the Child Welfare Board when they refused to follow Commissioners

Court policy to reduce county funding of $2.5 million to the state Child Protective Services agency. We wanted to use the funds to help stabilize families so they could keep their children. We replaced some board members and appointed a new chairman who supported our efforts.

Our metropolitan transit agency (VIA) was moving at a snail's pace in implementing new technology, on-demand services, and alternative means of transportation. When the county's board appointees did not respond to our concerns, we removed all of them and appointed new members. Finally, VIA targeted a large section in the northeast part of town to implement on-demand services and vans for transportation.

Appointed commissions and agencies have a habit of taking on a life of their own, ignoring the commissioners and City Council policy. Keep the broom ready to make board changes.

63

PREPARE FOR A LANDSCAPE COVERED WITH BONES OF BROKEN FRIENDSHIPS.

In 1988 when Mayor Henry Cisneros changed his mind and announced he wanted to run for re-election to a fifth term after all, many of his long-time friends refused to back him and instead they supported former mayor Lila Cockrell.

Broken hearted, he said, "But these were my friends."

Councilperson Helen Dutmer responded to Henry, "I told you they would do this to you... use you and then throw you away."

Friendship in politics is over-rated because it is in fact a fair-weather friendship. The political system is too volatile to have many true friends. Friends abandon you in the heat of battle if they think you will lose. They make donations to you and your opponent as well. They will also turn on you when you don't give them an appointment or contract they sought. Even if you have done them a favor in the past, it is not good enough. They are looking for what you can do for them in future.

There are some telltale signs when they are thinking about betrayal. Be leery when a friend starts a sentence with "Frankly," "To tell the truth," "Honestly," or "In all candor." He or she is probably fixing to stick it to you.

When I ran for mayor, a good friend of mine resigned as my treasurer when he got pressure to support Mayor Cockrell. I then appointed another friend and he too resigned when I criticized VIA, of which he was a board member.

As mentioned in *Principle 12*, we acted fast to build the county's first all-digital library before the city could build up political pressure to stop us. After opening the first location in 2013 several of my friends joined city library officials and supported my Republican challenger the following year. This was in spite of the fact that when I was mayor, my wife Tracy raised $5 million, and I added to $5 million in new city funding to build and open the new San Antonio central library. As county judge I also supported the San Antonio public library with funding of $3.8 million annually.

My friend, architect Henry Muñoz, supported my 2014 primary opponent because I did not vote for a contract he wanted with the county.

In the 2014 general election my friend, the late businessman Red McCombs, who owned an empire of car dealerships, supported my Republican opponent because I advocated for a streetcar system.

Oscar Wilde famously said, "A true friend stabs you in the chest." Not so in politics, where friends stab you in the back when you least expect it.

While you keep an eye on your political opponents, keep both eyes on your friends. President Harry Truman said, "If you want a friend in Washington, get a dog."

They now say you need two dogs because one will eventually tear your pants leg off.

But don't feel too bad because friends of your political opponents will do the same thing to them. Their betraying friend can be of use to you. I have received political donations from Republicans even when I had a Republican opponent.

Try not to get depressed as you step over the landscape of broken friendships. With a few exceptions that's just the way it is.

64

DANCE WITH THE DEVIL IF HE WILL BRING GOLD TO YOUR CITY.

Most people are devil dodgers, never wanting to get close to Lucifer. But remember, although the devil may scare you, he cannot kill you, so dance with him if he can bring gold to your city. If you are up to successfully dancing with him and bringing gold to your city, you will be perceived as a potent, red-blooded hero.

Boxing promoter Don King once killed a man in self-defense, and then later went to prison for stomping another man to death over a gambling debt. When he got out of prison, he climbed up in the boxing world to become its greatest promoter, managing great fighters such as Muhammad Ali, Mike Tyson and Julio Cesar Chavez.

In my third year as mayor in 1993, King was considering venues to host a championship bout between junior welterweight world champion Julio Cesar Chavez (87-0 at the time) and welterweight champion Pernell Whitaker. My advisors and friends warned me not to dance with King because he would drag me and the city down under.

Throughout my life, I had met all kinds of hustlers playing poker. Through poker, I learned how hustlers think and I managed to out-maneuver most of them. I also found out there is honor among hustlers if they think you are up to their game and you treat them with kindness.

So, we softened King up first. I sent a police escort to pick him up at the airport. Then my wife Tracy and I had dinner with the big man with spiked hair, booming voice, and penetrating eyes. I agreed to introduce him to the business community, help promote the fight, and make our 65,000 seat Alamodome available. We now had a relationship.

Later, he announced the fight would be held in San Antonio. I spent a lot of time with King as we promoted the fight. I also got to know Chavez and jogged with him along with his trainers.

Now here is how the devil works. After jogging with Chavez, I told King that he seemed out of shape. I said if he lost, our predominantly Hispanic audience could get violent.

I then asked, "Is he going to win?"

Don answered, "I don't know who is going to win but I know who is not going to lose."

I responded with a smile.

On the night of September 10, 1993, every expert in the fight business thought that Whitaker had won. But the scorers called it a draw and Chavez and Whitaker both retained their respective titles. That is how the devil works.

We filled the dome with close to 70,000 people, making it the 10th largest attended boxing event in history. Thousands of media members came to San Antonio. Hotels, restaurants, and retail shops prospered. San Antonio got the gold, and the devil went home.

If you know how to deal with the devil, he can bring riches to your city if you are up to dancing with him.

65

REFUSE TO DANCE WITH SPORTS HUSTLERS, THE HANDMAIDENS OF BEELZEBUB.

Don King knew he was the devil, I knew he was the devil, and so did everybody else. He owned up to it and did not try to disguise it.

Out of town major league franchise owners, who say they want to move their team to your city, come in the disguise of gentlemen, oozing with sophistication, pedigree, education, and money. They are in fact the handmaidens of the Prince of Darkness, not as powerful but more treacherous.

They know the public clamors for the gladiators of NFL football, NHL hockey, NBA basketball, Major League Soccer, and Major League Baseball. They also know their stable of athletic stars have become our present-day heroes, taking the place of authors, explorers, scientists and soldiers.

In August 2005 after Hurricane Katrina hit New Orleans, Saints owner Tom Benson agreed to have his football team play three games in our Alamodome while New Orleans was recovering from the devastation and cleaning up. At the first game he told Mayor Phil Hardberger he wanted to move the Saints to San Antonio. Hardberger bit hard and announced he would pursue the Saints.

Some four months later, Benson announced the Saints would stay in New Orleans. He had used us to get the state of Louisiana and the city of New Orleans to rebuild their Superdome and give him a sweetheart deal.

A few months later MLB Florida Marlins baseball president David Sampson called me and said they were definitely moving the baseball team and it was only a question of where they would locate. Even the president of Major League Baseball, Bob DuPuy, assured me that the Marlins were serious.

Blinded by the love of baseball, I spent four months wooing them, and offering to help finance the building of a new stadium in San Antonio. I finally came to my senses and realized they were playing me. I withdrew my offer.

They lied when they said they were moving. Instead, three years later they got the city of Miami to build them a new stadium. By the way, they came in last in attendance in 2019. They deserved to be last.

In 2017, Major League Soccer said they would add four franchises. Spurs Sports and Entertainment Group thought we would be a favorite to win one of the four franchises, so they filed an application. The city and county bought a soccer stadium from developer Gordon Hartman who had fielded a minor league team. We leased the stadium to the Spurs, and they fielded a team in the United Soccer League.

After the Spurs applied for a franchise and after the city and the county bought the stadium, we discovered that MLS officials had failed to tell us that Anthony Precourt, franchise owner of the Columbus, Ohio team, had a hidden clause that authorized them to relocate to Austin, just 75 miles from San Antonio, which meant if they put a team in Austin, they would not put a new franchise in San Antonio. Making matters worse, Anthony Precourt was on the selection committee for new franchises.

In a clever move they gave Austin a new franchise even though Austin did not apply for one. Anthony Precourt is chairman of the Austin ownership group. This was by far the most underhanded action by a major league organization that I have ever encountered.

About the same time as the soccer debacle, the Oakland Raiders played the San Antonio card too. City officials danced with them and offered up the Alamodome. Based on my previous experience, I said they were lying, and it made the newspaper in Oakland. The Raiders were not too happy, but it turned out to be the truth when they moved to Los Angeles.

If your city has a sports franchise, concentrate on supporting them. When I was mayor in 1994, we built and opened a new baseball park for the double-A San Antonio Missions. It was a jewel of a park, seating 6,500.

In 2000, Bexar County Judge Cindi Krier won voter approval to build the San Antonio Spurs the AT&T arena *(Principle 13)*. In 2008 while I was county judge, voters approved county bonds in the amount of $75 million for upgrades to the arena.

For the last 20 years, the Holt family has had a controlling interest in the Spurs franchise and has invested substantial funds to build a winning team. Under their leadership, the Spurs have been the NBA World Champion five-times. They have also invested over $100 million in a new human performance center that will open in 2023.

Sometimes you have to take a little political heat. Because we are a small market town with few large corporations, Chairman Peter J. Holt developed a plan to expand the reach of the Spurs franchise by attracting regional corporate and fan support. He wanted to play five "home" games away from the AT&T Center: one in the Alamodome, two in Mexico and two in Austin.

Many citizens did not like the idea, fearing they may move the team to Austin. I thought otherwise and led the Commissioners Court to approve the five games for one year. The games were a great success and the Spurs started selling more seats in the Spurs arena and attracted more advertising. My successor Judge Peter Sakai extended the five games for another year.

By the way, Holt picked the winning lottery number in May 2023 and drafted Victor Wembanyama, a once in a generation player. He joins former first picks David Robinson (1987) and Tim Duncan (1997). We are on our way to another championship.

Our United Soccer League team continues to play in the city/county stadium we bought for them. They won the championship in 2022 and have on several occasions beat MLS teams. As of May 2023, they have not lost in the last 23 games and draw full-house crowds to every game. To hell with MLS.

In 2023 the city and county are now working with a new group of local owners who took over the San Antonio Missions baseball franchise in 2022. Our baseball stadium is nearing 30 years old and needs substantial upgrades. With our booming downtown of tourists and residents, the new owners continue to work with city and county officials to build a new stadium there.

Don't take the bait of sports hustlers trying to use your city to get a better deal elsewhere. Support and invest in your own local professional teams.

66

DON'T HACK OFF STRAIGHT-SHOOTING GUYS WHO CARRY SUITCASES OF MONEY.

It is not wise to unnecessarily provoke a powerful guy with bucks and political smarts who can take dead aim at you. If you do not check your ego at the door and properly assess your potential adversary, you may not recognize the danger coming your way.

In 1996, Mayor Bill Thornton tried to get CPS Energy (owned by the city of San Antonio) to compete against Southwestern Bell (now AT&T) by using their cable lines to provide internet services. We had just brought SWB's corporate headquarters to San Antonio two years earlier when I was mayor.

So naturally, Southwestern Bell CEO Ed Whitacre felt betrayed and loaded up his six-shooter with cartridges of gold coins. He put his money, name, and prestige behind Councilman Howard Peak, who went on to defeat Thornton in 1997, as mentioned in *Principle 59*. Thornton picked an unnecessary fight with Whitacre.

In the 2011 legislative session, San Antonio Republican Senator Jeff Wentworth took campaign donations from the conservative tort reform alliance and then voted against them. He was not prepared for their upcoming retaliation.

The tort reform guys did not tolerate answers from politicians who take their money and then say things like, "Let me think about it" or "I can't be with you on this one." They spent $1 million to defeat him in the 2012 Republican primary.

In 2022 former Republican County Commissioner Trish DeBerry in her race for County Judge picked a fight with wealthy personal injury attorney Thomas J. Henry and CEO of the PM Group Bob Wills. Without any evidence she charged them with funding a dark money campaign that ran negative television commercials about her. She also said that Henry had a problem with women.

Henry responded full throttle on October 6 with a huge media conference in front of the courthouse. Standing with dozens of women he called Trish a liar. It was all downhill for Trish after Henry and Wills moved in with a hard-hitting response.

If you do pick a fight, pick one you can win and make sure you have the funds to offset the big buck guys. I was successful in my fight with the business establishment during my mayoral campaign because I invested my own personal funds.

Don't pick a fight with guys who have bucks and know how to deploy them. But if the need is great, make sure you have enough jingle-jangle in your pocket to offset their resources.

67

STREAMLINE AN APPOINTMENT PROCESS.

When you appoint someone to a political office, the losing applicants and their friends will not be happy. To hold down the angry list I set up an expeditious appointment process. It decreases the pressure on the court/council and puts the appointee on the job quickly.

I set up a process that gave ten days for someone to apply from the date of posting. I then had staff quickly narrow the list down to no more than three who would be interviewed. We voted on the same day after we did the interviews.

During my two terms as mayor, one councilman resigned in 1991, two in 1992 and one in 1993. After the interviews we quickly appointed four new council members who were equally divided between women and men.

While serving as county judge we appointed judges in 2002, 2012, 2015 and 2018. In a bipartisan approach, we appointed two Republicans and two Democrats.

By having a tight timeline at the City Council and Commissioners Court, we held down the number of people who were disappointed that they or their candidate did not get appointed.

Leaving a vacant seat empty for a long period of time is also not fair to constituents. In 2023 the council delayed for a month an appointment to name an interim replacement for District 7 Councilperson Ana Sandoval when she resigned.

It was also not fair to the applicants because council members knew they would appoint Rosie Castro, the renowned civil rights activist and mother of Congressman Joaquin Castro and former Mayor Julian Castro. She was eventually appointed but the council district had no representation for a month because of the delay.

In almost all cases we made a good appointment using an expedited appointment process. But good or bad you can also expect some ungrateful SOBs. After we appointed John Longoria a county court-at-law judge, he signed a letter with me that supported bail bond reform. Then as I sat down for a meeting with the judges, he handed me a letter reversing his position, and spoke against the reform at that meeting.

After appointing Republican Tom Rickhoff as County Probate Judge, he ran against me in 2018, launching a nasty personal attack campaign. Republican Justice of the Peace Jeff Wentworth (the former state senator mentioned above) whom we appointed, supported Rickhoff.

In 2013, at the behest of Commissioner Paul Elizondo, we appointed Queta Rodriquez as the Bexar County Veterans Services Officer. In 2018 she ran against Paul, who had health challenges. Paul won, but it took a lot out of him, and he passed away a few months later.

As County Judge I had the sole authority to appoint a person to the Commissioners Court when a vacancy occurred. In 2019, after my great friend colleague Commissioner Paul Elizondo passed, I appointed State Representative Justin Rodriquez, a Democrat to take his place.

In 2022 after Republican Commissioner Trish DeBerry surprisingly filed for County Judge on the last filing day, she agreed to hold over as commissioner for a month giving me time to find a good Republican. I appointed former Fourth Court of Appeals Judge Marialyn Barnard, a Republican. By the way, they were both great appointments and always treated me with respect.

Don't drag out the appointment process. Instead set a reasonable timeline for applicants and interviews and then decide. Appointing a qualified person to office is important, but in most cases there are no political wins.

68

BEWARE, THE HUNTER CAN BECOME THE HUNTED.

There are 26 suburban cities in Bexar County. For some strange reason in 2019 political turmoil reigned in four of the suburban City Councils and in the Commissioners Court when we all sought to remove an elected official.

In 2019, Leon Valley Mayor Chris Riley and her City Council removed Councilman Benny Martinez for allegedly violating the city charter. Then Martinez' supporters collected signatures to recall two councilmembers who voted for Martinez' removal. Later, charges were filed against Mayor Riley for unethical behavior. In 2021 Martinez ran for election and won. The hunters became the hunted.

In July 2019, at instigation of some of the council members, Castle Hills police arrested Councilwomen Lesley Wenger and Sylvia Gonzalez for felony charges relating to fraudulent use of identifying information and tampering with a government record. The district attorney found there was insufficient evidence to prosecute. Wenger and Gonzalez sued the city.

In October, the Mayor and City Council of Converse voted 4-1 to remove Councilwoman Kate Silvas for requesting voluminous documents from staff without first contacting the City Manager, a violation of the city charter. But a few weeks later a judge issued an order re-instating her.

In a different twist, city of Cibolo councilmembers sought to remove their mayor, Stosh Boyle, because at age 21 he had been convicted of a conspiracy to manufacture the drug ecstasy. The removal failed and in November 2019 Mayor Boyle became the hunter and won re-election.

Bexar County Constable Michele Vela Barrientes engaged in several wacko incidents such as a warrantless blood draw from a teen and extracting cash for security from a citizen at one of our county parks. She was also accused of harassment and retaliation against some of her own employees.

After the FBI raided her office on September 23, 2019, she announced for sheriff. I invoked the "resign to run" provision of a state statute and took steps to remove her from office. Her lawyer got a temporary restraining order but then a judge lifted the restraining order.

The Commissioners Court then removed her from office and appointed 25-year deputy sheriff veteran Leticia Vazquez. Vela continued her campaign against Sheriff Javier Salazar, but she lost.

In January 2023 Barrientes was convicted of two felony accounts of tampering with records. She received five years of probation and 90 days in jail. In this case the hunter prevailed.

If you are going to overturn voters' choice of an elected official, you'd better have the goods or you will become the hunted.

69

FIGHT THE STATE FOR LOCAL FREEDOM AND AUTHORITY.

There was a time in Texas when Republicans supported local authority, letting citizens of cities and counties chose their local leaders in elections and then authorizing them to determine what ordinances, budgets, and projects they needed to benefit their local community.

But, as the large cities of Texas became dominated by Democrats, Texas Republican legislators in recent legislative sessions have done their best to abolish local control.

In 2015, Republicans removed the right of local officials to control oil and gas drilling related activities. In 2017, they pre-empted cities from regulating ride-hailing companies. They made local officials subject to punishment for violating anti-immigration measures. They passed numerous voter suppression measures.

As mentioned previously, Republican House Speaker Dennis Bonnen in 2019 said his goal was to make this the worst session in the history of the legislature for cities and counties. He became the engineer of a freight train loaded with Republican votes against local government. In 2019 they set spending limits on local government. We were able to slightly moderate the effect of the spending cap by getting debt excluded.

In 2021 it got darker when the legislature enacted more voting restrictions in the form of voter ID requirements. In 2022, they made it harder for senior citizens to vote by mail. Over 20 percent of mail ballots in Bexar County were rejected in the first election in Bexar County after this, because of the confusing conditions that were imposed by the state.

They say it is always the darkest right before it goes absolutely pitch black. Near pitch black came upon us during the legislative session of 2023. Republican bills passed that targeted progressive district attorneys and judges, intimidated voters by increasing criminal penalties for violating voting restrictions and prohibited local mask mandates during a pandemic such as the COVID-19 crises.

The most devastating passed bill was described by some as the "Death Star." The bill prevented City Councils from passing ordinances related to codes if they were more restrictive than what was specifically authorized. The codes included business and commerce, labor, finance, insurance, natural resources, occupation, and property codes. Depending on the interpretation of the bill, it could prohibit the city from prohibiting loud music from clubs that disturb neighbors, ordinances that protect the Edwards Aquifer from overuse, and payday lending restrictions.

The Houston City Council filed a lawsuit contending it effectively violated the city's self-governance as described in the state constitution.

Over the years we have fought back against the state. On June 26, 2017, I testified in federal court against Governor Greg Abbott and Lt. Governor Dan Patrick. They had passed a law that sought to remove local public officials for not following a new state requirement to question people about their citizenship. I stated in court that the law was unconstitutional and that both of them should be removed from office for voter suppression. We prevailed in court. During the COVID-19 crises Governor Abbott's emergency orders restricted local officials' efforts to contain the spread. We fought back with lawsuits and won a few victories.

We have held demonstrations, filed lawsuits, sought federal help, and campaigned against far-right Republican members of the legislature. While we have had some victories, we are slowly losing the struggle. If the legislature keeps chipping away the right of local authority and freedom, then local government will in effect be taken over by the state.

But if we keep fighting, one day the oppressive restrictions on local freedom will be overcome. At 83 years old I am not sure I will be around when that day comes.

Citizens should have the right to choose their local leaders in elections and then authorize them to determine what ordinances, budgets, and projects are needed for their community. To preserve that right, you must fight back against a state government that seeks to abolish local authority and freedom.

COMMUNICATE WITH KNOWLEDGE, TRUTH AND CLARITY

70

BECOME AN ATTENTION MERCHANT.

To gain power and make things happen, being a wallflower simply will not get you there. You must become an attention merchant by recreating and continually renewing yourself to achieve dominant visibility.

But not in the way former President Donald Trump divided our nation. Nor in the way Theodore Roosevelt did, by wanting to be a bride at every wedding and a corpse at every funeral.

You must gain positive attention by getting things done and being out front and becoming a bragger-in-chief for your council/court. If you successfully dominate, everyone begins to spin off you. Do not expect to get credit when things are going swell. As one journalist told me, "We do not cover airplanes that land safely."

But if something goes wrong, and they often do, the media will jump on it. Therefore, you must generate sustained publicity on quality accomplishments and initiatives that will offset negative stories.

Mayor Henry Cisneros dominated the political life of San Antonio during the 1980s with his looks, smarts, communication skills and his aggressive agenda. He had that rare animal-like charisma and sold his soul to politics. He was everywhere, selling his major projects: a new central library, a domed stadium, literacy learning centers, and numerous other projects.

Mayor Phil Hardberger (2005-2009) catapulted to a high attention level when he led the effort to help refugees who came to our city after Hurricane Katrina hit Louisiana. He capitalized on the positive attention he created as a caring mayor and used it to push forward major projects such as the redevelopment of the northern "Museum Reach" of the San Antonio River.

Mayor Julian Castro (2009-2012) picked up the attention mantel with his media charisma when he gave a rousing speech at the Democratic national convention in 2012. As an attention merchant, he sold increased taxes for Pre-K to the public and revitalized inner-city housing with incentives totaling $75 million.

You must also be willing to stir it up by tackling controversial issues that will get you a lot of attention. I loved to stir it up with issues I really believed in, while realizing I would also pick up detractors in the process.

Many times, I spoke out against a city/state Alamo redevelopment plan that would have closed the historic plaza in front of the church, thereby preventing the historical and highly popular annual Battle of Flowers parade from passing in front of it, and not preserved the historic 1929 Woolworth building located across the street.

Finally in March of 2021 Mayor Ron Nirenberg and the City Council supported the changes that I advocated. I got a lot of attention when I persuaded the Commissioners Court to fund $25 million toward preserving and converting the Woolworth Building into part of a world class Alamo Museum *(Principle 45)*.

Mayor Nirenberg and I got even more attention when we

had 319 media briefings during the COVID-19 crisis *(Story in Principle 28)*.

My long tenure, having served in five different political offices, has led to the perception that I had more power and influence than I really had. What the public perceives becomes reality in their eyes, and that translates into real power.

Without a spotlight you will not be able to be an effective leader. Turn it up a notch and don't be afraid to speak out.

71

DRESS WITH SARTORIAL SPLENDOR.

It does not take long for a person to size you up. Those first few moments can be critical in a person's assessment of you. You are, in a sense, what you wear and how you carry yourself. People will take notice and judge you accordingly.

As mayor and county judge I wore a suit, tie, and laced shoes five days a week. My most powerful look was a solid, navy blue suit with a white shirt, blue or red tie, and laced dark maroon shoes. I also wore a sky and sea classic blue suit with a light blue tie that evoked nature and a pinstripe blue suit with a solid blue tie.

After a blue suit, my next favorite was a solid grey and a pinstripe grey along with a purple tie and black shoes. Occasionally I wore a brown suit with light blue stripes and a tie that picked up the blue.

On some days when I did not make public appearances, I wore a sport coat, a tie, and slacks. At weekend events, I wore an open collared shirt with sleeves rolled up and jeans. No, I did not look uncomfortable.

During the winter, I wore a fedora hat made by Borsellino. In the summer, I wore a fedora style Panama hat made in Ecuador.

Ladies were very much attracted to my hats and said so. It added to the attention merchant image.

As my sight began to diminish, I started wearing bi-focal glasses, giving me a more studious look. Forget reading glasses. Taking them off and on is irritating to watch.

The frame for your clothes is important, so I stayed trim and strong by lifting weights, jogging, and not overeating.

In my appearance I have left no doubt in constituents' minds that I have the strength and swagger to carry on for quite some time, even as I moved into my eighties.

Icons are signs of power, and your body is your most powerful icon. So, keep your body in shape and dress it properly.

72

JUMP ON NEWSPAPER STORIES.

When I was mayor in 1993, the Hearst Corporation, which owned the *San Antonio Light* newspaper, bought the *San Antonio Express-News*, owned by Rupert Murdoch. In an ironic twist, Hearst closed the *Light* and kept the *Express-News*. San Antonio joined the ranks of big cities in America with only one newspaper.

Since 2014, more than one in five newspapers across the country have shuttered. Consequently, local newspapers no longer have the impact they once had.

But, while circulation is down, newspapers are still read by the influential political, business, and civic leaders. They are the power groups that seek to determine public policy, as well as elected officials' futures.

Newspaper stories are in-depth and thoughtful, backed up by careful and thorough research. *Express-News* editorials provide a good analysis of hot local political issues. So, I read the *Express-News* daily, looking for issues to tackle.

In addition, I read the digital *San Antonio Report*, a nonprofit in the style of the *Texas Tribune*. I also read the daily *Wall Street Journal* and the Sunday edition of the *New York Times*.

After I wove the information I gathered into a proposed new policy, I built public support by then turning to the electronic media: television, radio, and social media, where the majority of people now get the news.

As one constituent sarcastically told me, "You never let anyone get between you and a camera."

He was right. I do not believe you can get enough electronic coverage unless, of course, you have really screwed something up and the media has you for lunch.

The following are examples of how I have used newspaper information to formulate policies that I then sought to accomplish.

In 2015, I followed up on articles in the *Wall Street Journal* regarding the high sugar content of sodas. We created an eye-catching ad that featured a person swallowing 20 packs of sugar, the amount of sugar in a 20-ounce soda.

In 2017, after reading a series of stories regarding the evolving opioid crises in the *New York Times*, I led Bexar County to sue the pharmaceutical companies for misrepresentation. In 2022 we settled with several of the companies and began to receive millions of dollars.

In March 2019, I responded to *San Antonio Express-News* editorials on criminal judicial reform by taking on the bail bond industry, criminal defense attorneys, and judges who were doing injustice to minorities and the less fortunate *(Story in Principle 31)*.

In 2021, when I read the *San Antonio Report* about the plight of immigrant children entering the United States, I reached an agreement with the federal Department of Health and Human Services to house them in county facilities *(Story in Principle 78)*.

You will only find timely well researched stories in quality daily newspapers. Take advantage of the stories from which you can develop new policies.

73

MONITOR AND ANALYZE MEDIA COVERAGE.

Bexar County public information officer Monica Ramos contracted with Meltwater, the world's first online media monitoring company, to monitor and analyze the media coverage of our news releases and media conferences. She also tracked the effectiveness of our social media sites.

Her tracking told us how effective the various media outlets were and what segments of the population they were reaching. It also told us what the public was interested in and what they were thinking about our message.

On July 30, 2019, at our media conference we announced that Bexar County would be one of the first two Texas counties to go to trial in the opioid lawsuit against the pharmaceutical companies. Meltwater's analysis showed that 189,844 people saw the story in the *San Antonio Express-News*. Our four local television stations had a total of 514,831 viewers of the news conference, of which KSAT television alone reached half of the television audience, 254,398 people. The balance picked up the story on radio and specialty news outlets.

Television news dominated the newspaper 2-1. Our message reached a total of 1,061,514 people, which is a significant number in our media market.

We now knew we had a hot topic in the opioid lawsuit and interest would be high in future developments. We also knew that we needed to give KSAT a lot of love.

The county produces videos twice a month that are posted on the county's Facebook page. Based on our tracking and analysis we knew how many watched the videos and how many reacted with comments. We then pushed additional stories on topics they were interested in.

My Chief of Staff, Nicole Erfurth, monitored my posts on my social network site. In August 2019, I posted a letter that I wrote to the local Democratic party chairman opposing a proposed Democratic boycott of Bill Miller Bar-B-Q because one of the company's owners had donated to Donald Trump. While I opposed Trump, I did not think it was right to boycott the company that employs hundreds of people and makes large donations to local nonprofit organizations.

The letter reached 30,568 people, of which 9,795 engaged, and 1,497 commented. Out of those 1,497 comments, 1,444 agreed with my stance. This was by far my largest personal engagement on social media. I stopped the boycott.

By monitoring and analyzing your web site, news conferences and press releases you will learn what gets attention and what people feel about your actions. That information will tell you what you should be promoting.

74

BUY PAID MEDIA TO HIGHLIGHT YOUR MAJOR PROJECTS.

At best, citizen attention is fleeting. Stories come and go every day as you seek to highlight the positive. The only way to overcome the overload of daily information is to buy paid advertising. Sharp, focused, and sustained advertising will reinforce your hold on the public's attention.

Before buying paid media, we first publicized our accomplishments through news releases and media conferences. We staged media conferences in interesting places that provided good visuals to highlight our major projects. For example, we held numerous media events on San Pedro Creek and the southern reach of the San Antonio River which were beautiful backdrops.

After our successful trip to Bonn, Germany, where our four missions and the Alamo were inscribed as a World Heritage Site, we held a media conference when we returned home on July 6, 2015, in front of the Alamo. We celebrated what was now the only world heritage site in Texas.

We assembled those clips from the media conferences to create a paid media spot highlighting the major projects. We developed catchy commercials that appeared repeatedly in various media outlets.

For example, along with the San Antonio River Authority, we developed a fun and lively paid media spot that showed me walking down the 8-mile Mission Reach of the San Antonio River, joined by children, bikers, high school students, and seniors as music played. The spot highlighted the county's investment in the restoration of the river and drew thousands of people to the river.

We advertised our remodeled Bexar County Coliseum and the new 350,000 sq. ft. exhibit halls that we built. We bought media to advertise our new $900 million University Hospital and downtown ambulatory care building. We bought paid media to tout our investments in helping people during the COVID 19 epidemic.

Paid media is necessary to draw citizens' attention to new major capital projects and to highlight your accomplishments.

75

IN A PUBLIC SHOWDOWN, EI CARRIES THE DAY OVER IQ.

Experts say we have emotional intelligence (E.I.) capable of recognizing our own emotions and those of others. They have also found that our emotional intelligence allows us to guide our behavior to achieve our goals and that E.I. is twice as important as your Intelligence Quotient (I.Q.)

For sure, in a political showdown, E.I. almost always carries the day over I.Q. When presenting a proposal for voter approval you must motivate, provoke, urge action and be energetic and confident. It is best to use the two most powerful emotions: compassion, and fear.

Citizens Against Virtually Everything (often referred to as CAVE people) know what they do not want, but they do not know what they want, so they fight against every proposal. They look for an election hoping to find one every week, so they can stick it to you.

Research has shown that ads trying to change their minds by rational argument will not work. So, in an election that you are required to call you must turn want into need by evoking compassion or fear or both to turn out your vote as well as to stymie your opposition.

In May 2008, we passed a $414 million county bond issue by evoking both fear and compassion. We evoked fear of youth crime if we did not provide safe alternatives for youths by building 13 amateur sports facilities. We evoked fear that the 5-time world champion Spurs might leave San Antonio if we did not upgrade our arena. We played on fear of flooding if we did not improve flood control and restore the Mission Reach of the San Antonio River. We played on compassion that the Bexar County Performing Arts Center would provide musical education for 85,000 children each year.

We won all four propositions by wide margins by evoking emotions to turn out our vote.

In 2012 when Mayor Castro went to the voters to raise the sales tax for Pre-K education, he evoked a message of compassion to overcome the fear of new taxes. He developed a television ad featuring the teacher of the year, a young Hispanic female, who was surrounded by children. He carried the day with the emotion of compassion embedded in the ideals that all our youngest citizens deserved to start with quality education.

In 2018, Mayor Nirenberg used fear to win over voters to oppose a proposition that would require only 20,000 signatures instead of the 75,000 required by the city charter, to call an election to overturn an action by the City Council. He warned that San Antonio would become like California where special interest groups called numerous elections that led to bad public policy.

At the same election he won the vote on the petition issue on fear, he lost two other issues, capping the city manager's salary and enacting an eight-year term limit and a collective bargaining issue. From the city perspective he was unable to use fear or compassion or any emotional issue. Instead, the fire union used the compassion issue of unfairness in the high pay of the city manager and the unfairness of the collective bargaining process.

Since 2018, under the existing city charter there have been five petition-initiated city charter amendments. Citizen groups are feeling more empowered and becoming more active working for a variety of changes.

Be prepared in a political showdown to use the power of emotion. People vote their emotions more than any intellectual analysis of an issue.

76

DON'T OVER-REACT TO THE "PRECAUTIONARY PRINCIPLE."

There is a theory is that if a proposed event is a low probability, but with a high impact, you should respond aggressively, including giving warnings. It's a great theory but hard to apply.

After the September 11, 2001, terrorist attack on our homeland, federal officials kept issuing warnings about possible future attacks. The unverified false alerts caused unnecessary disruption and resulted in a lack of confidence in government. The government finally stopped giving them warnings.

I made a mistake about warning when an envelope with powder and a picture of Osama bin Laden on it was found in our City Hall. It turned out to be a hoax. It was coffee creamer instead of anthrax.

After a record rainfall event in 2002, I went on television and said that people living below the Medina Dam in Medina County, located just west of San Antonio, should vacate their homes when the water behind the dam had reached 18 inches from the top. The dam has no spillway and experts feared it could collapse if it were overtopped. The water level never went any higher and I was subsequently roundly criticized for crying wolf. Even t-shirts were made with a wolf howling.

Learning from my mistakes, I stopped over-reacting with warnings and instead focused on preparation for the possible event and letting people know what we were doing.

In 2014, an Ebola patient died in Dallas, only 300 miles from San Antonio. We did not send out warnings, but rather brought all our emergency people together at a press conference and laid out a plan if an Ebola case occurred locally. We were able to assure the public we were prepared. No local cases of Ebola developed.

When the COVID-19 pandemic hit our community in 2020-21, Mayor Nirenberg and I gave updates and advice each night on our television show based on information from health experts. We never over-reacted with constant warnings. We simply told people the facts when COVID cases started rising and what people needed to do to protect themselves.

If a high impact event has a low probably of happening, don't cry wolf. Instead assure the public you are prepared to handle the potential occurrence. Use preparation instead of verbal overheating.

77

KNOW WHEN TO SHUT UP.

It is hard to say "no comment" when asked a question by the media. The media does not like it, the public does not like it, and you feel like you should say something.

But there are times to shut up. One answer can lead to another question and then before you know it you are running down a deep rabbit hole of responses you did not intend to make.

In 1988, I announced I was withdrawing from the mayor's race because the time was not right for me *(Story in Principle 4)*. When the media pressed questions about my private life I responded, "no comment." If I had answered one question, I would have started my descent.

In *Principle 59* I mentioned that Republican Judge Tom Rickoff was my opponent in 2018. During the campaign he personally attacked my wife and me. I was ready to strike back with a throat punch, but my political consultant, Christian Archer, told me he was an ankle-biting pest and that I should not interrupt him while he was making a mistake and embarrassing himself with his unsubstantiated charges. So, I kept my mouth shut, ignored him, and whipped him 58.9 percent to 39 percent.

In 2022, former District Judge Peter Sakai ran against Republican former County Commissioner Trish DeBerry to succeed me. She called him "Dr. No" to emphasize how he voted against some initiatives. It was interpreted as an ethnic slur against a Japanese-American candidate as the voters remembered the villain in the 1962 James Bond movie. She also attacked his judicial record. He kept his cool, did not respond, and won the election with 57 percent of the vote.

So, remember there are times when it is in your best interest to keep your mouth shut. An uncontrolled loose hinge can get you in trouble.

78

RESCUE TRUTH THAT IS SHOVED INTO THE ABYSS OF SOCIAL MEDIA.

On January 25, 2019, Republican Texas Secretary of State David Whitley sent county election officials a list of 98,000 naturalized Texans who had registered to vote and instructed them to immediately contact all of them, require proof of citizenship, and take action to remove any non-citizens within 30 days.

Texas Attorney General Ken Paxton then blasted a "Voter Fraud Alert" over Twitter and vowed to prosecute. President Trump tweeted and said that these numbers were the tip of the iceberg. Before you knew it, tens of thousands of people picked up the social media tweets and shared them.

After meeting with Bexar County Elections Administrator Jackie Callanen, I announced that we would not comply with the order. Too many times in the past Republican state officials have tried to disenfranchise voters. I smelled another rat.

Later federal Judge Fred Biery ruled there was no evidence of voter fraud and that the people on the list should not be contacted. The state agreed to drop the plan and paid $450,000 to the civil rights lawyers who sued them. In June, through open records, it was found that Governor Abbott had initiated the whole debacle.

On April 6, 2021, Governor Abbott and two Texas Rangers, an arm of the Department of Public Safety (DPS), appeared in front of the Bexar County Expo Hall where we were providing temporary housing for 2,100 migrant boys aged 13-17 who were seeking asylum. Governor Abbott made outrageous allegations including child assault, understaffing, that they were not being fed properly and that children with COVID-19 were not separated from others. He called for closing the center down without any credible evidence. The lies spread across social media, bringing additional criticism of our operation.

I had to wait until the investigation was concluded and then I said on April 28 that Governor Abbott's claims were completely false. I said it was a horribly dehumanizing political stunt by the governor. The story made the front page and was picked up by social media.

While truth finally prevailed in the voter suppression case and Abbott's lies about the immigrant center, truth is not always going to win. Before social media, lies were short-lived because they had no wings, but now they have large vulture wings.

Researchers at the Massachusetts Institute of Technology in 2018 found that false stories on Twitter travel six times faster than truth and reach a lot more people. This does not count false stories from bots and cyborgs. The venom of lies no longer evaporates.

Robert Kennedy Jr, who has announced for the Democrat nomination for president in 2023, has spread conspiracy theories and lies all over social media. He has been active in the anti-vaccine movement, saying they caused autism. He also suggested that Ann Frank and the Jews in Germany had more freedom than American citizens because some businesses mandated COVID-19 vaccines during the crisis. He called COVID-19 a bioweapon that was somehow ethnically targeted and engineered to spare the Jews and the Chinese.

As a result, the information age has become the disinformation age, leading to an unraveling of truth and a polarization of the community. The abnormal becomes the normal in a nation that is going a little crazy.

And it is going to get worse with the advent of the new power of artificial intelligence being able to create fake messages, video and audio that look and sound realistic. In an election these tools can be used to create fake images and voices of candidates. Get ready for the 2024 presidential election.

As Supreme Court Justice Oliver Wendell Holmes wrote in his dissenting opinion in the case of Abrams vs. United States (1919), "The best test of truth is the power of thought to get accepted."

To overcome lies you must first develop a covenant with citizens that is based on respect, not just popularity. If you are successful, you have created a living dynamic relationship where truth can prevail. But you are not always going to win because false stories spread faster than wind-blown seeds, no matter how hard you push truth.

You must fight back, pounding away on true facts and refuting the half-truths and lies. Through speeches and public appearances, I pushed truth. I also used my website, Facebook, Twitter, and e-mail blasts to push the truth using short, emotional, pithy phrases.

In some cases, public service does not work out so well for those who tell the truth. Sometimes you pay the ultimate political price, you either lose an election or you are forced out of politics. Many Republicans who stood up to Trump's false claims lost their re-election. But that is the risk you must take.

There is hope that at least the traditional media will quit spreading lies. Dominion Voting Systems accepted $787.5 million from Fox News in April 2023 as damages for the spreading of lies about their voting machines during 2020 presidential election.

Fox, led by demagogic host Tucker Carlson, had repeatedly spread wild conspiracy theories about fraud in the presidential election. He endorsed Trump's view that Dominion was rigging the election while at the same time he disparaged them in private texts to colleagues. A few days after the settlement announcement Carlson was let go.

But unfortunately, The United States Supreme Court found in May 2023 that Twitter, Google, and Facebook were not liable for hosting terrorist material on their sites. The court held that section 230 of the 1996 Communications Decency Act shields social media from liability for user-generated content. The law needs to be changed to hold social media like Fox News accountable.

Today the power of truth is facing its greatest threat to being accepted. You must stand up and fight for truth, or else lies, conspiracy theories, and distortions will prevail, leading us down the road to a failed nation.

79

SAY WHAT YOU HAVE TO SAY AND GET OUT OF THE WAY.

One day before I gave my first State of the County address to the Greater San Antonio Chamber of Commerce, I asked then chamber president Joe Krier how long I should speak. He answered, "Well, I have never had anyone come up to me after a speech and say, 'I wish that fellow had talked a little longer.'" I got it.

So, I always tried to keep my speeches to about 20 minutes. Even at the 19th minute, I caught a few eyes glazing over, and knew tomatoes were only a few minutes away. In speeches that were not a major address, I usually kept them down to five to 10 minutes long. While restraining length, it is also important to have little umph and zip to your speech. I have found that speaking from a prepared text comes across as stale and boring. I might share a great deal of knowledge, but who in the hell is actually listening?

So, I speak extraneously from an outline of major topics that keeps my presentation from becoming disjointed. I also consciously speak from my diaphragm rather than from my throat, giving me a much more powerful voice and timber. I try to inspire my audience with words of power, using declarative sentences with action words, much like Hemmingway wrote. I start my speeches by outlining major challenges that we face. I end with a challenge to act decisively on my proposals.

I also acknowledge the work of colleagues, calling them out by name. It gives them recognition that they deserve, and they appreciate the shout out.

I speak as if I were talking across the table to someone. By looking around the room, I connect with everyone. Sometimes I touch ideas buried somewhere in me and they come tumbling out.

I do not use mealy-mouth expressions like, "...but what if," "...maybe," "...on the other hand," "...I don't know what to think," "...although," "...despite," "...otherwise," and "...I'm not sure about that." Instead, I speak in plain language, using short clear words.

Again, think Hemingway.

I love it when a person, after hearing some of my earthy language, says to me in a joking way, "Tell me how you really feel."

I state clearly what projects I want to accomplish and what issues I want to address.

I know what has worked before and what has died as soon as the words left my lips. I practice the speech several times before my staff to get the right cadence and timing. I use humor and personal experiences to keep the speech informal and meaningful.

There are good days when I will really connect with the audience and get them enthused. On those days, I establish a dialogue with my audience knowing they feel what I feel. I have connected.

On bad days, malapropisms creep in and my humor does not work. But even on a bad day, I come across better than reading from a prepared speech.

The media often covers my speeches, and my off-the-cuff remarks make it easier for them to extract good quotes.

Speak with clear words and passion, leaving no doubts about where you stand on issues. Long-winded boring speeches lead to naptime for your audience.

81

DON'T SMOKE AND MIRROR
A CONTROVERSIAL PROPOSAL.

In 2004, Mayor Ed Garza thought he had a clever plan to get voters to approve extending term limits, raising council pay and providing employee benefits to City Council staffers who were contractors rather than employees. He decided to sugarcoat the three issues with a fourth issue, establishment of an independent Ethics Review Board. He thought voters would pass the other three issues if they knew an independent board would scrutinize the council.

Unfortunately, the voters saw through the smokescreen and defeated term limit extension, council pay and staff employee benefits by a 69 percent margin. The Ethics Review Board passed with 71 percent of the vote. The Council had to become more ethical without the opportunity to make a decent salary that would make them less reliant on political contributions.

For five years, I attempted to gain support for a streetcar initiative by painting it with rosy colors, and never admitting its shortcomings such as the disruptive construction time and the impact on vehicle traffic. People saw through the smoke and stuck it to me.

In 2019, Mayor Nirenberg and the City Council moved to

delete Chick-fil-A from a list of new airport vendors recommended by staff. The mayor said he voted against Chick-fil-A because they are closed on Sundays. Everyone knew the real reason was because the owners opposed same sex marriage.

A lawsuit was filed. Finally, in September 2020 the city acknowledged their inappropriate action and reached an agreement with the Federal Aviation Administration to offer Chick-fil-A a location in the San Antonio International Airport. Chick-fil-A then declined the offer.

Voters are smarter than politicians give them credit for. People will forgive you for disagreeing with them, but if they see you are doing a snow job they may not be so forgiving.

You are better off fessing up, instead of obscuring up. Light will find its way through foggy clouds of obscuration.

82

STAY OUT OF AN ECHO CHAMBER.

It is so easy to be stuck in an echo chamber where you are only hearing the echo of your own voice which you have always been in love with. And that voice can lead you down to the path of vanity which is the sum of false humility, proselytizing, and pretentiousness.

People say nice things about you, they smile, give you a hug, and clap when you finish a speech. You feel good about yourself, listening to the chorale sound of the crowd who you believe share your own thoughts. The lilting sounds of repeated compliments assure you of your greatness.

But the guy that slaps you on the back, smiles, and claps for you when you make a speech does not mean he is on your side. If you could only hear what they say to their friends when they walk out...

I was caught in an echo chamber in 1974 when I ran for Congress while I was serving in the Texas Constitutional Convention. I was chairing the most important committee that was tasked with assembling the constitutional articles for a final convention vote. I was full of myself from all the compliments I had received. Because of my work in the convention, I never set foot in half of the counties in my district. I lost the congressional race.

We then failed by three votes of a super majority to submit a new constitution to the voters. The next legislature picked up our work and submitted the eight articles of the proposed constitution. On April 22, 1975, all of them lost. A triple whammy and I was drummed out of office for the next 13 years after leaving the Senate. The price of vanity can be very high.

Mayor Lila Cockrell was caught in an echo chamber in 1991, thinking she was too popular to be beaten. Everyone around Mayor Ivy Taylor in 2017 assured her that her good record would pave the way to re-election. Both lost their re-election.

Commissioner Tommy Adkisson said that he had never had so much positive affirmation as when he decided to take me on in my 2015 re-election campaign. I won by 57-43 percent.

Best to listen to the voices of the opposition to understand what vulnerabilities you may have. My wife Tracy has her ear close to the ground and warns me about any growing criticism. She helps me stay out of an echo chamber. Most of the time.

Politics is a game of deception. If your head is not clear enough to see through acclaim and praise, then you will cruise along a road of delusion that could lead to your defeat.

83

ACCEPT NO SLIGHT OF YOUR PUBLIC OFFICE.

Any disrespect shown to the office of mayor/county executive diminishes that office. When I led a delegation to Guadalajara, Mexico, as mayor in 1991, a group of business leaders chose to go separately and create their own agenda. When I arrived, I told Governor Cosío Vidaurri that I was not happy with a business delegation that wanted to meet with him separately.

He said, "I will schedule a lunch with them and make them wait an hour and then we will walk in together."

When we walked in together, they realized their mistake about the importance of the office of mayor.

There are also rules I follow so that I am not put in a position that could demean the office of mayor/county executive. I do not want the office to be disregarded, embarrassed, or dismissed as unimportant. Here they are:

> *1. If invited to a civic breakfast, lunch or dinner do not go unless invited to sit at the head table out of respect for the office you hold.*
> *2. Do not let any organization roast you, as too often remarks*

meant to be funny are actually demeaning, inappropriate and offensive.

3. If funding a project, insist on proper recognition.

4. Demand restraint and decorum by citizens who speak at City Council/Commissioners Court meetings.

5. When invited to be part of an organized public effort, ask "How do I fit in?" If the role is not clear or meaningful, decline.

6. Do not go to meetings unless you are fully aware of who is attending and what their agenda is.

7. Don't participate in talk radio shows that have a political agenda.

8. Don't argue with people who are a quart low, for they will pull you down to their level.

The office of mayor/county executive deserves respect and it's up to you to protect its integrity.

SET THE TABLE TO CREATE SMART JOBS

84

EXPAND AND DIVERSIFY YOUR LOCAL ECONOMY.

San Antonio had a narrow-based economy up through the 1960s, living mostly off its five local military bases. We took a first step to diversify when we held HemisFair, the 1968 World's Fair and International Exposition. It led to the building of the convention center and to a vibrant tourist industry.

During the time I served in the legislature in early 1970s, the University of Texas at San Antonio (UTSA) and the UT Health Science Center (UT Health) with its complex of medical-related schools were in the beginning stages of their development. Over the years UT Health led the way to a huge bio-medical sector. UTSA was instrumental in creating an educated workforce across numerous economic sectors, including engineering, technology, and advanced manufacturing.

These events set the stage for the city to further expand and diversify our economy. When Henry Cisneros was elected mayor in 1981, he became the first mayor of San Antonio to rank jobs at the top of the agenda. He created an Economic Development Department that offered city incentives for companies that invested capital and created jobs. He called on out-of-town companies to locate in San Antonio and led the effort to develop international relations with Japan and Mexico.

Every mayor since Cisneros has followed his path. As mayor in the early 1990s, I was successful in attracting the headquarters of Southwestern Bell, which later morphed into AT&T. After leading the local effort to pass NAFTA, I was able to secure the North American Development Bank to locate in San Antonio. Additional international companies followed.

Mayor Bill Thornton was instrumental in securing the land and buildings when the federal government closed Kelly Air Force Base in 1995. The city appointed a board to convert the base into what is now Port San Antonio, with 80 businesses employing 15,000 workers. A strong aerospace industry has been built around Boeing and StandardAero. The Port also has the largest concentration of cyber security firms in San Antonio.

Mayor Howard Peak was instrumental in acquiring the land of Brooks Air Force Base, in southeast San Antonio, in 2002. It became "Brooks City Base" in an effort to keep the base open by reducing the cost of operating it. Those efforts failed. But Mayor Ed Garza acquired the buildings when the base was finally closed in 2005. The city then created the Brooks Redevelopment Authority and now 50 private companies employ 3,200 workers and hundreds of apartments have been built there.

After becoming county judge in 2001 I created a county Economic Development Department to focus on advanced manufacturing that uses state of the art technology, a cornerstone of innovation in making things. Advanced manufacturing is integrated into a world economy that connects suppliers with manufacturers.

As mentioned in *Principle 18*, I led the effort to successfully attract Toyota and Navistar manufacturing plants. In 2022 Toyota invested $390 million in state-of-the art technology to enable different vehicles to be manufactured on the same line. At the same time Navistar opened an innovation center that will focus on designing new trucks.

Other advanced manufacturing firms have located in the San Antonio area, including INDO-MIM, Bakkovor Foods, Nissei America, Mission Solar, Aisin Texas, Caterpillar and Cuisine Solutions.

Today, manufacturing firms in San Antonio employ over 51,000 workers.

Our economy is now diversified with aerospace, automotive manufacturing, bioscience, tourism, cyber security, and a high-tech industry. Over a million people are now employed in Bexar County because we collectively focused on economic development diversity.

Partner with the private sector in diversifying and sustaining your local economy to create better paying jobs.

85

DEVELOP AND RECRUIT A SKILLED WORKFORCE.

While our five local colleges and universities generated engineers, scientists, and mathematicians who have critical thinking and communication skills, we did not fill the void of a middle-skilled workforce. Although the Alamo College District, through their five college campuses, offered skilled worker programs, they did not match the needs of many local employers.

So, in 2015 Mayor Taylor and I announced the founding of SA Works. Led by private employers, the organization developed a list of the various skills that their workers needed.

The Alamo College District responded by offering additional skill training classes. Private firms such as Codeup and the Cloud Academy along with Hallmark University provided additional skilled training classes and certificate programs. Companies paid for their employees to enroll in these programs and also developed on-the-job training programs, internships, apprenticeships, and job shadow days.

SA Works partnered with the local school districts to create skilled training programs for middle and high school students. Four CAST (Center for Applied Science and Technology) high schools have since been created. A cyber security and an advanced manufacturing high school have been created. Numerous other skill development programs have been started in other high schools.

Through Bexar County's Military and Veterans Service Center, we focused on recruiting skilled veterans who are transitioning out of military service to stay in San Antonio. We found them jobs and provided services to facilitate their transition.

In 2016, the county, led by Economic Development director David Marquez, initiated a two-year advanced manufacturing apprenticeship program in a partnership with 15 manufacturing firms and the Alamo College District. When students graduate, they are guaranteed a full-time job.

In 2019, Mayor Nirenberg and I co-chaired "Alamo Promise," a campaign to raise funds to pay student tuition and fees to attend one of the Alamo College's schools and obtain an associate degree or a certificate in a skilled job program. They now offer skill programs in 155 occupational categories.

Mayor Nirenberg took another major step forward and led the effort to convince voters in a November 2020 ballot initiative to approve an additional $174 million for job training.

In 2022 a report from the American Growth Project of the University of North Carolina ranked San Antonio seventh among the 50 largest metropolitan areas in the rate of productivity growth of our workforce from 2007-2022. We worked collaboratively to focus on the right path to developing the talent we need to attract companies, and retain and grow our local companies.

Middle skill jobs are critical to creating a strong, diversified economy. You must bring the business sector to the table to develop the required middle skilled worker training programs.

86

EMBRACE CREATIVE ARTISTS.

While we had embarked on successful skilled job training programs, we also recognized that artists are a key to having a talented workforce. They see the world through lenses that lead to better design of products and buildings as well as websites and software. The arts improve skills in problem solving, sequencing, team building, planning and organizing.

After becoming county judge in 2001, I teamed up with Mayor Ed Garza to co-chair an "arts collaborative" to expand the arts and document their economic impact. We wanted a more robust arts community to enhance the culture of our city as well as our economy. Over a two-year period, 1,000 citizens participated in the collaborative.

A study by Trinity University presented to the collaborative found that some 12,000 people were working in arts related jobs such as advertising, marketing, architectural design, digital marketing, and film production as well as the performing and visual arts.

The final plan developed by the collaborative included 38 specific goals. The city's Arts and Culture Department took the lead in working to accomplish the goals. During the process people began to understand that it takes creative artists to build a great city.

With the plan in place, I was able to convince the Commissioners Court to make large investments in the arts. We partnered with the private sector to create an arts organization known as "The Fund" to help nonprofit arts organizations. We also funded an arts internship program for students who worked for various arts organizations each summer. We made significant annual contributions to the symphony, ballet, opera, and other performing arts organizations.

We started a program to include artists in any new county construction projects. For example, the Bexar County Hospital District's new 10-story hospital and the 6-story clinical building included a budget of $9 million for works of art from 97 artists. Studies show that patients who have been exposed to art in the hospital show a healing benefit.

We commissioned numerous murals along the county's downtown San Pedro Creek project as we turned it into a new "cultural park." *(More on this in Principle 90).*

The county invested $110 million in the new Tobin Center for the Performing Arts (2008), $6 million in the new Briscoe Western Art Museum (2013), $5 million in the expansion and reconstruction of the Witte Museum (2018), and $10 million in the restoration of the historic Alameda Theater (2020). And in 2021, we committed $25 million to the building of a new Alamo Museum as part of a massive Alamo Plaza redevelopment project.

The arts are thriving, and artists are adding to our creative work force.

Artists enhance the culture of your community and provide talented members of the workforce. Cities and counties should step up to support the arts.

87

DISRUPT AND INNOVATE TO BREAK DOWN BARRIERS TO DIGITAL INFORMATION.

As I mentioned earlier, I formed a team of county staff and began plans to build the nation's first all-digital library. The following is how we focused on delivering digital literacy to those on the wrong side of the digital divide.

We developed a young, smart, technology-oriented staff and hired a skilled forward-looking librarian. We built a state of the art 4,000 sq. ft. digital library on the south side of San Antonio that we opened in the fall of 2013.

The digital library had an open workspace that included 40 large screen Apple computers connected to the internet. Along the side, we built study rooms and a children's center. We provided a large collection of e-books and audio books along with digital magazines, newspapers, and music.

We loaned out hundreds of e-book readers downloaded with books that patrons could check out and take home. Later we provided free Wifi hotspots that connected them to the internet at home. We had over 100,000 visits to our small digital library in the first year.

The cost to build, open and operate our digital libraries is approximately one-third of the cost of a traditional library. By concentrating on technology and digital information we were able to develop a highly-skilled staff that is preparing those without resources to enter the digital world.

Many of our patrons never enter the library because they can access all e-books, magazines, newspapers, comics, movies, and training on our internet web site.

Since then, we have built three more digital libraries and provided e-books and readers to 58 public school libraries, three military libraries, Bexar County's University Hospital, school buses and public transportation. We sponsor the yearly Newby Film Awards to students who make a one-and-a-half-minute movie from a book they read.

In 2022, we opened the first BiblioTech to serve a school. We renovated an existing building on the Fox Tech campus in the San Antonio Independent School District that will serve middle and high school students. It is larger than our other libraries, 8,000 sq. ft., and included a robotic center, a recording studio, a maker's space for art projects, a children's area, a large conference room and an outside enclosed garden.

To date over 1.4 million people have visited our website and over one million e-books have been checked out. We now offer over 500,000 e-book selections. We even offer special programs at libraries which over 100,000 patrons attend each year.

Digital literacy is necessary for workers to communicate, connect and collaborate. Be creative in seeking to help those on the wrong side of the digital divide by providing them free access to technology and digital information.

88

CREATE A TECH ECOSYSTEM.

We learned a harsh, but valuable lesson in the 1970s when San Antonio passed up an opportunity to create a tech ecosystem at a time when we were on the cutting edge of technology. Datapoint Corporation, founded in 1969, produced the first personal computers and went on to have great success creating thousands of jobs in San Antonio. In honor of the company the city named a street after them where several of the buildings were located.

But in the 1980s the tech world passed Datapoint by and eventually shoved them into the dustbin of tech history. All that is left is the street that was named after them. Unfortunately, we did nothing to attract and grow other technology companies in San Antonio.

We had our second chance in 1999 when the cloud computing company Rackspace was founded in our city. Two years after its founding, we created the San Antonio Technology Accelerator Initiative that I co-chaired with tech entrepreneur David Spencer. We focused on creating a diversified tech ecosystem to augment the success of Rackspace.

We first focused on cyber security by successfully lobbying the National Security Agency to locate a regional headquarters in

San Antonio. We also spent time in the Pentagon working with the Air Force to locate the Air Force Cyber Warfare Command to San Antonio.

We worked with UTSA to establish cyber security courses. Over the years, we have become the largest center for cyber security outside of Washington, D.C. Today we have over 100 private sector cyber security firms in San Antonio.

We took another step forward in 2011 when Graham Weston, the founder of Rackspace, created "Geekdom" in an historic former department store in the central city, a co-working space for tech start-ups. With incentives from the city and county, numerous other downtown buildings have been remodeled to include high speed fiber optic internet, common lounges, and recreational areas. Over 60 tech firms are now located in the central city.

In 2015, the Commissioners Court initiated a $1 million annual innovation fund to foster growth of small tech start-up firms. We gave grants to Easy Expunctions, FlashScan, SoHacks, Liquid Web, Digital Creative, Hut Group 381 and several other tech firms.

We have a growing diversified tech ecosystem that can provide cloud computing, digital advertising, cyber security, telemedicine, distance learning, meeting formats, software, web sites, and numerous other tech products and services.

A study led by David Heard, CEO of Tech Bloc, that was completed in the summer of 2022, found that there were 48,000 workers in information technology (IT) in San Antonio, earning an average of $87,000 as of 2020. They were employed by 1,491 technology companies as well as national security organizations. While the downtown area acts as the tech incubator, it has fewer tech jobs than Port San Antonio where most of the cyber security firms are located. The northside of San Antonio has a diversity of the tech firms.

Building a diversified tech ecosystem was critical because in the last few years Rackspace business has declined. As of December 2022, they were down to 700 employees and in March 2023 they announced additional layoffs. We still hope for a turnaround, but if it does not happen, we now have a strong tech industry even without them.

Team up with leaders of your tech sector to broaden the network of companies by offering incentives to start-up companies. Work your congressional delegation to bring home federal agencies that are leaders in technology.

89

BUILD TRANSFORMING PROJECTS IN THE URBAN CORE.

Transforming projects inspire a vibrant, cultured, and educated community as you weave them together to create a collective impact. They can change a community's trajectory, offering a new way of life and attracting a young, talented workforce.

In 2008, I teamed up with Mayor Phil Hardberger who took the lead to connect the downtown Riverwalk to the 22-acre abandoned Pearl Brewery site located just two miles north of downtown. With city and county funding in cooperation with the San Antonio River Authority, the San Antonio River was restored with landscaping, walking paths and public art.

The river investment led to local entrepreneur Kit Goldsbury redeveloping the Pearl's abandoned buildings into a hotel, restaurants, and retail space along with new construction that included apartments and office buildings. Thousands of additional apartments and offices were built in the vicinity.

Mayor Julian Castro (2012-2015) provided funding and a plan to redevelop the 92-acre HemisFair Park, site of the San Antonio's 1968 world's fair. A children's park, restaurants, housing, a hotel, retail, and office space have been or are being built. A green garden-like "civic park" located in the northwest corner of the site opened in 2023.

In 2014, we opened the Tobin Center, a state of the art performing arts center. It is located on the downtown San Antonio River leading to the Pearl redevelopment.

In October 2022, we held the grand opening of the downtown restored San Pedro Creek, funded by the county in the amount of $230 million. Our common thread of humanity is told through interpretive signs and murals along the creek.

The creek project has transformed the west side of downtown. Texas Public Radio, UTSA's new six-story data science building, a new federal courthouse, new apartment buildings, new headquarters for the San Antonio Independent School District, and a new Frost Bank tower are all located on San Pedro creek. The historic Alameda Theater, also located on the creek, is also being restored by the city and county.

All these projects link together an urban core that offers a lifestyle that is attractive to a young, educated workforce. More millennials moved to San Antonio from 2010 to 2017 than any other city. In 2021, we led the nation in the total number of people who moved to our city.

Keep the inner city heart beating. Invest in the core of your city to offer a vibrant urban lifestyle that will attract a young, educated work force.

90

RESTORE, PRESERVE, AND ENHANCE FAUNA AND FLORA.

Our prehistoric ancestors had it right when they lived in kinship with their environment and worshipped the spirit of the river and nature. It is important in urban centers that open spaces, parks, rivers, and creeks are preserved and enhanced. They offer a safe green haven away from the hustle of city life.

When I was mayor in 1992, the city partnered with the Edwards Aquifer Authority to purchase 5,510 acres in northwest Bexar County from the Resolution Trust Corporation. It had once been the site of a proposed new town but was acquired by the RTC when the saving and loan industry collapsed. It was a rare and beautiful natural tract of canyons, creeks, meadows, and open spaces. There are even tracks of dinosaurs who roamed across the land some 110 million years ago during the Cretaceous period.

Over time, more acquisitions were made bringing the total to 12,240 acres. Government Canyon is now a state natural area and is the largest nature preserve located next to any American city.

As mentioned earlier, I led the county effort to provide $200 million in funding for the restoration of the 8-mile southern

"Mission Reach" of the San Antonio River leading from downtown to Mission Espada. We created 13 acres of wetlands, 113 acres of aquatic habitat, and 334 acres of riparian habitat. More than 10,000 pounds of native grass and wildflower seeds of more than 60 species were planted. Twenty thousand trees and shrubs including more than 40 native species were also planted. Recreation features include hike and bike trails, picnic sites, pavilions, and adjacent city and county parks.

Access portals were built on the river connecting to the four Spanish missions. We have set aside a total of 2400 acres of open space, three times the size of Central Park in New York. We completed the project in 2013. It is the largest environmental restoration of an urban river in the United States.

Near the southern reach of the river is Mitchell Lake, which had once been a sewage disposal lake. Starting during my term as mayor we began the process of cleaning it up and converting it into an internationally recognized bird sanctuary. It is also the site of a local Audubon Society interpretive center.

The downtown restoration of San Pedro Creek included enlarging the creek way. Water quality and aquatic habitat were improved. Aquatic plants and trees, shrubs and grasses have been planted alongside the creek and walkways. When finally completed the restored creek will lead to the confluence with the Mission Reach of the River.

In 2007 Mayor Phil Hardberger had the city purchase 300 acres of land in the middle of the fast growing north side. He created an ecological park with walking paths along with a land bridge over the Wurzbach Parkway which is a unique arterial green highway, to connect both sides of the park.

In 2014, then-councilman Ron Nirenberg strung together

funding from various conservation groups to acquire 1,521 acres to protect the Bracken Bat Cave. It houses the world's largest Mexican free-tailed bat colony. Adjacent to the site the county purchased and set aside 1,700 acres as habitat for the golden cheeked warbler, an endangered bird species. That land connects to another 800 acres that we set aside adjacent to the Marriott resort property. Four thousand contiguous acres are preserved forever.

Mayor Howard Peak was instrumental in starting the restoration of Salado, Leon, Olmos and west side creeks, with pathways eventually extending 84 miles. In 2021 the county funded $244 million for additional restoration and trails along the creeks. The funding will add an additional 34 miles, creating a unique necklace of parks throughout the county.

In 2021 former Mayor Cisneros asked me to support his vision to build an arboretum to celebrate the miracle of trees whose leaves clean the air of carbon dioxide and allow us to breathe. I had been to the arboretum in Houston and was excited about the project. In 2022 I included $7.2 million in the county budget for the arboretum. Henry found the perfect place, the abandoned 180-acre Republic golf course, and made arrangements to buy it. He created a foundation and was off and running.

Together the city and the county have created one of the greenest communities in the country.

Nature provides us a safe haven, cleans our air, and beautifies a city. Cities and counties should protect it, enhance it, and preserve it for future generations.

91

INVEST IN GOVERNMENT ECONOMIC GENERATORS.

When I was mayor in 1992, we created the San Antonio Water System (SAWS) by consolidating three different water related agencies. We established a nine-member City Council appointed board.

Since then, SAWS has invested in a desalination plant, an underground storage reservoir for surplus Edwards Aquifer water, and implemented a robust water recycling system. Under the leadership of SAW's CEO Robert Puente, they have also built a pipeline to bring in additional water from Burleson County, 140 miles northeast of San Antonio. Along with diversifying our water supply, they have also established an effective conservation plan.

The City of San Antonio acquired a small electric and gas utility in 1939. Since then, CPS Energy has grown to become the largest municipally owned utility in the nation. It serves approximately 850,000 electrical customers and 350,000 natural gas customers. It generates its own electrical power using coal, natural gas, nuclear, and renewable resources such as wind and solar. They are presently in the process of decommissioning one of their coal-fired generating plants.

SAWS and CPS Energy have fostered economic development by giving low bulk water and energy rates to businesses. As a result, several manufacturing and data centers have located in San Antonio. Together they both also provide the city of San Antonio a revenue source of approximately $400 million each year.

When I became county judge in 2001, the Bexar County Hospital District was in serious financial trouble. I decided to focus on turning it into a first-class hospital. I first held a health care summit that adopted measures to increase federal funding and develop a working relationship between private hospitals and our county hospital, which is now called University Hospital, in recognition of its status as the teaching hospital for the adjacent UT Health Science Center.

At the same time, I set about stabilizing the hospital district's finances by increasing their property tax revenue. Within four years, the hospital district became solvent. In 2005 the seven-member Board of Managers (three appointed by the county judge and one by each of the commissioners) selected George Hernandez as CEO. George was a forward-looking leader willing to take entrepreneurial risks and I was ready to help him.

In 2008 the Commissioners Court took a quantum leap by approving a tax increase and authorizing approximately $900 million in debt to finance a new state-of-the-art, one-million-square-foot, ten-story hospital and a six-story clinical and surgery center.

Since the opening of the new hospital and clinical building in 2014, our business increased by 50 percent and our hospital district has become a powerful economic engine. Several outstanding specialties have been developed, such as organ transplants.

In September 2017 the Commissioners Court approved $450 million to build a 550,000 sq. ft. children and women's hospital next to our new hospital. It opened six months after my term ended in the summer of 2023.

In July 2022, the Commissioners Court authorized $500 million in certificates of obligation to build two community hospitals, one on the northeast side of town and one on the south side, next to the Texas A&M University campus.

The hospital district now has 10,000 employees that work in a sprawling network of clinics, research institutes, outpatient surgery centers, and the new hospital and clinical building.

With a $3 billion annual operation, our Bexar County Hospital District along with the University of Texas Health Science Center, led by President Bill Henrich, continue to drive the health care industry. Private firms such as Gally International Biomedical, Optech, CeloNova BioSciences, Phoenix Biotechnology and Acelity are thriving.

As of 2020, our health and bioscience industry has created over 200,000 jobs, employing nearly 1 in 5 local workers, and generated $42.4 billion in sales. In the past decade, the industry has increased its economic impact by 74 percent.

I mention in *Principle 46* that Mayor Nirenberg and the City Council took the first steps toward a much needed improvement and expansion of the San Antonio International Airport. The $2.5 billion project includes an extension of the airport's principal runway and construction of a new terminal bigger than the two existing terminals, and a ground loading facility.

The project is critical to meeting the needs of our expanding population. Between 2010-2020 the San Antonio metro area grew by 400,000 people. In 2022 about 9.5 million passengers traveled through the airport and this figure is expected to grow to 14 million by 2040.

But the project is subject to the city successfully attracting grants from the Federal Aviation Administration. I am optimistic and look forward to its completion in the years ahead.

An entrepreneurial spirit should not be limited to the private sector. Invest in new government economic generators and expand existing ones. They will act as a catalyst to creating more jobs in the private sector.

SET A
TIME
TO LEAVE

92

LEAVE AT THE TOP OF YOUR GAME.

In early 2021, I saw a picture in the *Wall Street Journal* of an aging senior executive being wheeled out of his office on a dolly with a potted plant in his lap. It was a profound statement, and I did not want to become him.

I also remembered the story of Conservative MP Leo Amery telling Prime Minister of the United Kingdom, Neville Chamberlain, "You have sat here too long for any good you have been doing. Depart, I say and let us have done with you."

Chamberlain resigned not long after, on May 10, 1940.

I was at the top of my game when I saw that *Wall Street Journal* picture in 2021. Even though some of my hopes were shredded and some of my aims missed the mark, all my major initiatives were completed or near completion.

After serving in political office for over 33 years, the thrill of political life had diminished, and the rhythm of my life was starting to repeat. If I hung around, I also knew my performance in the game I had been winning could deteriorate and frankly, so could I. I did not want to become a shadow of myself or be forced out or end up like the guy on the dolly.

I remembered how difficult it was for Mayor Henry Cisneros to leave office. In 1989 on the day of his last council meeting in emotional terms he said, "I would love to stay. It's difficult for me to go back to private life."

It may have been difficult for Cisneros, but it was the right time for him to leave because he left at the top of his game. Had he stayed longer he would have faced a slowing economy and a time when activists gained the upper hand and imposed the most stringent term limits on the mayor and council.

I was a subject of terms limits when I became mayor, so I had no choice of when to leave, but as county judge I could go on and on as long as I won re-election.

I had won my last county judge race in 2018 by 18 points and as the 2022 re-election approached, I looked like a cinch with my poll numbers consistently exceeding 60 percent approval.

By summertime, I decided when and how I would say goodbye.

Don't wait for the downside. Don't wait for the dolly. Don't hang around to be pushed out. Leave when you are at the top of your game, while you are under no pressure to do so.

93

A LONG GOODBYE IS BEST.

On October 5, 2021, I closed my state of the county speech before the Greater San Antonio Chamber of Commerce by announcing I would not run for re-election after serving five terms as county judge. I made the announcement early because it would allow time for good candidates to step forward. The primary elections were six months away, followed by the general election another seven months later.

It allowed me plenty of time to finish my major projects that were close to completion. It also gave me time to provide for the transition of my staff and to publish a book I was writing on the COVID-19 crisis. In addition, I had time to undertake some new short-term initiatives and organize my archives and find a home for them.

It's a myth that a lame duck cannot get the job done. During the long goodbye, we completed the downtown section of the San Pedro Creek and passed a $619 million bond package that funded a parks master plan that included 34 miles of creek improvements and numerous road and flood control projects. We funded a $30 million building for the newly created public health division of the Bexar County Hospital District and $10 million for a public health school administered by UT Health and UTSA. We provided approximately $10 million for a new Preventive Health and Environmental Services Department and $35 million for mental health.

The long goodbye also gave time for numerous organizations to recognize me and my wife Tracy for public service, dating back 51 years to when I was first elected to the Texas Houses of Representatives. Over 20 events were held in our honor.

By the way, you can catch a life size bronze sculpture of Tracy and me on San Pedro Creek.

Announce early that you will not run for election, giving ample time for candidates to emerge and time to complete some of your major projects.

94

GET A NEW NAME.

The dethroned King Richard II lamented in Shakespeare's play, "I have no name... and know not now what name to call myself."

Once out of office, your life is diminished to ordinariness, your influence predeceases you, and your opinions go with you. Your successor does not want you around because there is no room at the top for two. You are now yesterday's man. Once a prince, now a frog.

When my phone stopped ringing, I considered taking sham calls. Not very many people acknowledged me at the HEB grocery store. I struggled like Richard II with what to call myself. Poor me.

I could no longer give the answer that State Senator Frank Madla once gave a constituent when he asked, "May I call you by your first name?"

Madla said, "Yes."

The constituent addressed him as Frank.

Madla replied, "Senator is my first name."

Without a name you may seek to go back home and reclaim your first name. If that thought enters your mind, think about

Thomas Wolfe's book *You Can't Go Home Again*, which was published posthumously in 1940. It is the story of George Webber, who tries to return home and finds out he does not fit in. He decides he must go forward rather than back to the past.

Going back home usually brings sadness, regrets, and unhappiness. Even if you are successful in regaining your office, you may find home not so inviting. Former president Teddy Roosevelt was unsuccessful in trying to go back home. Former Mayor Lila Cockrell left office, came back later to win again, but had an unsuccessful term and lost re-election.

Like George Webber, leave the past alone and go into the future, whatever that may be. If you cannot stand being nameless, then seek another office. President Clinton appointed Henry Cisneros Secretary of Housing and Urban Development and later President Obama appointed Julian Castro to the same office.

I got a new name when I left office on December 31, 2022. I picked up the name "professor" when I entered into a contract with my alma mater, St. Mary's University, to lecture and work with their students at the law, business and public administration schools. I also contracted with UTSA to do the same with their schools of liberal and fine arts, public health, and political science.

After leaving office chart a future for yourself leaving the past behind. If you can't get a new name, be happy with your birth name.

95

WRITE TO HAVE THE LAST SAY.

While institutional immortality spans the ages, most mayors and county executives will be forgotten. Your term of office will be lost in the fog of time because no one will have the full story of what you accomplished. Writers and historians may tell a smattering of your accomplishments, while others may get it all wrong and some, who may not be too fond of you, will make you stink.

I might add it also gives you a last opportunity to settle some old scores. So, write to have the last say.

After serving in the legislature and the constitutional convention I wrote a book *Challenge of Change*, documenting the day-to-day work of the convention.

After serving as mayor, I spent two years writing a book called *Mayor: An Inside View of San Antonio Politics, 1981-1995*. I started with Henry Cisneros' election in 1981 and went through my time as a councilman and then two terms as mayor. Today it is still read, mostly by young professionals interested in participating in local government. It is also used as a reference by the newspaper on many stories they write.

Trinity University Press published *Transforming San Antonio* in 2008 and *Changing the Face of San Antonio* in 2018. The two books cover 10 major projects that were developed from 2001 to 2020.

In 2015 I wrote the book *Bexar BiblioTech*, the story of how we created the country's first all-digital public library.

In 2019, my wife Tracy and I wrote a book *Restoration of the Bexar County Courthouse*. It tells the story of how we funded and led the effort over 22 years to restore the Bexar County Courthouse.

In 2022, Elm Grove published *The Mayor and the Judge*. The book covered the two-year war against COVID that Mayor Nirenberg and I led.

Now this book. There will be more to come.

So, write to have the last say. It's therapeutic, enjoyable, and will leave future generations valuable information and hopefully lessons that will be helpful to them.

AUTHOR NELSON W. WOLFF

Nelson Wolff was a founder, together with his brother George and his dad, of Alamo Enterprises, a building materials store that established eight locations in San Antonio and South Texas. They sold the company in 1978 to a national corporation.

In 1979, he and his brothers, George and Gary, along with Ron and Don Herrmann, founded Sun Harvest Farms, a natural foods supermarket that became a nine-store chain in central and south Texas. They sold that company in 2000 to another national corporation.

Wolff has served over 33 years in public office. He served in the Texas House of Representatives and the Texas Senate in the 1970s. From 1987 to 1995 he served two terms as a City Councilman and two terms as mayor of San Antonio, the seventh largest city in the United States.

He was appointed Bexar County Judge (the top executive officer in Texas county government) in 2001 and was re-elected five times. He chose to not run for a sixth term and completed his term of office in December 2022.

A *San Antonio Express-News* editorial on December 30, 2022 said Wolff had redefined county government and that "...he retires from political life as the most consequential public official of the modern San Antonio era."

He has written eight books and co-authored one book with his wife Tracy, the founder and chairperson of the Hidalgo Foundation. Together they have six children and eight grandchildren.